WORDS THAT WORK
Motivational Interviewing Mastery

How Even a Novice Can Consistently Cultivate a Commitment to Change and Multiply Client Success Rate In Health, Nutrition, Fitness, and Psychology

Alec Rowe and Jane Kennedy

© Copyright 2023 - All rights reserved.

The content contained within this book may not be reproduced, duplicated or transmitted without direct written permission from the author or the publisher.

Under no circumstances will any blame or legal responsibility be held against the publisher, or author, for any damages, reparation, or monetary loss due to the information contained within this book, either directly or indirectly.

Legal Notice:

This book is copyright protected. It is only for personal use. You cannot amend, distribute, sell, use, quote or paraphrase any part, or the content within this book, without the consent of the author or publisher.

Disclaimer Notice:

Please note the information contained within this document is for educational and entertainment purposes only. All effort has been executed to present accurate, up to date, reliable, complete information. No warranties of any kind are declared or implied. Readers acknowledge that the author is not engaged in the rendering of legal, financial, medical or professional advice. The content within this book has been derived from various sources. Please consult a licensed professional before attempting any techniques outlined in this book.

By reading this document, the reader agrees that under no circumstances is the author responsible for any losses, direct or indirect, that are incurred as a result of the use of the information contained within this document, including, but not limited to, errors, omissions, or inaccuracies.

TABLE OF CONTENTS

Introduction 1

Chapter 1 5

The Power of Words 5

   History and Evolution of Motivational Interviewing 6

   The Core Elements of Motivational Interviewing 9

   Principles of Motivational Interviewing 11

   Benefits of Motivational Interviewing 13

   Is MI Really Effective? 13

   Some Things to Consider 15

Chapter 2 17

The Role of the Coach 17

   Who Is a Coach? 18

   Traditional Coaching Versus MI Coaching 19

   Building a Collaborative Coaching Relationship 21

   The Role of Empathy in Coaching 25

Chapter 3 31

Techniques for Effective Motivational Interviewing 31

   Core Motivational Interviewing Techniques 32

   Unpacking Client Motivations 38

   Identifying and Handling Client Ambivalence 40

   The Stages-of-Change Model 41

Chapter 4 46

Motivational Interviewing in Fitness and Exercise 46

   Boosting Self-Efficacy for Building a Lifelong Practice 46

   Tackling Some Other Barriers to Physical Activity 51

Chapter 5 54

Motivational Interviewing in Nutrition and Weight Loss 54

    Addressing Common Barriers to Healthy Eating 55

    Assessing Your Client's Motivation for Change 56

    Creating the Decisional Balance Sheet 58

    Reflective Listening and Problem-Solving 59

    Helping Your Client Be Receptive to Change 61

    A Realistic and Empathetic Approach to Body Image Concerns 61

Chapter 6 66

Motivational Interviewing in Psychology 66

    Benefits of Motivational Interviewing for Mental Health 67

    Using Motivational Interviewing to Help Your Client Navigate Life's Twists and Turns 67

    Encouraging Your Clients to Challenge Their Negative Behavioral Patterns 69

    Use of Motivational Interviewing in the Treatment of Substance Abuse Disorders 71

    The FRAMES Approach in Motivational Interviewing 74

Chapter 7 77

Measuring Success and Evaluating Outcomes 77

    Importance of Measuring Your Client's Progress 78

    Different Measures of Success for a Motivational Interviewing Coach 81

Chapter 8 84

Building a Successful Coaching Practice 84

    Ensuring a Smooth Transition Into Motivational Interviewing Practices 84

    Identifying the Common Roadblocks You Might Face on Your Coaching Journey 87

    The Importance of Continuous and Lifelong Learning in Motivational Interviewing 89

Conclusion **91**
References **99**

Introduction

A person is a fluid process, not a fixed and static entity; a flowing river of change, not a block of solid material; a continually changing constellation of potentialities, not a fixed quantity of traits. –Carl Rogers

Whether you've been a coach for some time—or you've just started your coaching journey—you'll likely notice how much your clients both desire and despise change. They might truly want to achieve a goal and might even be working toward it for years, yet, something within them keeps them from achieving those goals. This isn't just limited to your client; it is equally applicable to you. Within each of us, we carry both the ability and the resistance to change. Take, for example, Susan.

Susan had been trying to adopt a "healthy eating" lifestyle for years. She knew that her current lifestyle made her feel lethargic, moody, and perpetually hungry. She knew that a diet consisting of less processed foods and more whole foods would not only help improve her physical health, but also do wonders for her mental and emotional health. When her coach Samantha met her for the first time, she was struck by how self-aware Susan was and how driven as well—at least on the surface. As she got to know Susan better, she realized that Susan usually lost weight quite easily, but it was challenging for her to maintain her weight loss. Over the years, this had led to a pattern of weight cycling—which was not only unhealthy but also dangerous for her health.

For Samantha, Susan's case posed a unique challenge. Susan also mentioned that she didn't have a great record with coaches because she found them too demanding or instructive. The problem, Susan emphasized, wasn't that she didn't know what needed to be done. It was that she could not find a sustainable plan that could bring about a lasting change in her lifestyle. At this time, Samantha had been learning motivational interviewing skills and decided to put them into practice.

She decided to let Susan drive their discussions forward by asking her open-ended questions and practicing reflective listening. Samantha took special care to not let judgment overpower her discussions and practiced empathy at all times. When Susan became comfortable in Samantha's presence, she was willing to open up and dig deep into her own motivations for—and resistance to—change. Together, they identified various barriers to lasting change—including Susan's emotional responses to stressful situations, her relationship with food, and her self-image. They came to the surprising conclusion that Susan was so used to looking and feeling a certain way that any change—even if it was a positive one—made her engage in self-sabotaging behaviors so that she could return to her "equilibrium" state.

This breakthrough enabled Samantha to work with Susan and create a plan that took into account Susan's emotional and behavioral tendencies. This plan also helped her tackle Susan's limiting self-beliefs in a way that she embraced change and became comfortable in her new lifestyle. Over a course of six months, Susan was able to lose almost 60 pounds. What's more, she was able to successfully keep this weight as well. After seeing how successful motivational interviewing was in helping her client—and thus, her business—Samantha decided to adopt it as a significant aspect of her coaching practice.

As a coach, you might be motivated by the desire to create a lasting positive impact on your clients, and to be known as a trusted professional in your field. At the same time, you might be aware of the challenges that you face as a coach. For some, it might be difficult to achieve lasting behavioral changes in their clients. For others, it might be difficult to create a coaching style that is inclusive and mindful of the different cultural backgrounds of their clients. For many of us, it becomes extremely daunting to build a solid practice and attract new clients in an industry that is fast becoming oversaturated. How do you convince your clients that you can offer them something that others can't, and that you have their well-being in mind at all times? It might also be difficult for some of us to keep ourselves updated with the latest trends in the coaching industry. Not only that, but how do we determine what works and what doesn't for our clients when we're too busy playing catch-up? All of these challenges can take a toll on our professional as well as personal lives.

The reason I'm writing this book is that I've been in your place and grappled with these very questions at one time. I was almost on the verge of burning out when I started learning about and applying motivational interviewing skills to my coaching practice. I want you to experience the same benefits that I received as a coach, such as:

- **Learning skills that are scientifically proven:** These skills are practical and actionable, and are scientifically proven to be effective. Through this book, you should be able to gain the confidence to use these techniques in your regular coaching practice.

- **Focus on behavioral change:** Motivational interviewing goes beyond generic phrases like "I have faith in you" and "You can do it." It helps the client delve deep into their own thought and behavioral patterns, and motivates them to change these behaviors once and for all.

- **Better results in limited time:** If you're a busy professional, chances are, you don't have the time to go through multiple videos and books to start your motivational interviewing practice. This book offers a concise yet comprehensive look into this practice, and also helps you avoid some of the most common pitfalls that coaches make in the beginning.

- **Improved client relationships and greater success rate:** Motivational interviewing places a lot of emphasis on empathy, reflective listening, and centering the client's life experiences. This helps clients have faith in you as a coach and also improves your success rate with them. The techniques discussed in this book will eventually help enhance your reputation as a coach.

- **Business growth:** Through this book, we will also discuss how to integrate motivational interviewing into our coaching practice, and to use it to attract and retain more clients in a competitive market.

- **Greater versatility as a coach:** The techniques related to motivational interviewing can be applied in a wide range of fields—including but not limited to fitness, psychology, nutrition, and sports. Adopting these techniques in your practice will help you gain experience with different kinds of clients and work with challenges that are unique to their scenarios.

- **Improved personal relationships:** Coaching can often be a demanding job, which means that many coaches struggle with maintaining proper work-life balance. Not only that, but they might feel like their professional commitments sometimes jeopardize their personal relationships. The techniques discussed in this book can be applied to both your professional and personal life, and can also help you relieve stress and enjoy greater work-life balance as a coach.

Motivational interviewing not only transformed my coaching practice, but also helped me gain control of my personal narrative. I sincerely hope that this book does the same for you.

Chapter 1
The Power of Words

Words have been around for almost as long as humanity, and they have played a huge role in shaping history. We use words to convey an entire range of feelings, develop connections with others, and express our own needs. With the popularization of social media, more and more people have the platforms they need to express themselves. As such, we're always confronted by the words of someone or another—and yet, most of it doesn't stick with us. There are only two types of speech that have a profound impact on us—one that is extremely vile and negative, and another that is positive, inspirational, and healing in nature.

Think about the last positive speech that affected you deeply. It doesn't even have to be from another person; think of the last time you spoke kindly or graciously to yourself. Think of all the things about that speech that stayed with you. What resonated deeply with you? What was so inspirational about that speech? What makes a speech impactful to someone can differ from person to person, but there are some commonalities among all of them.

What is even more intriguing in today's world is how most of the "positive" and "uplifting" speech we hear doesn't do anything for us. They seem flat or uninspiring, or even lazy and generic. In some cases, they might even come off as insincere. While overtly negative speech is obviously a turn-off, so too is speech that isn't authentic. As we start our journey of motivational interviewing (MI), it's extremely important to first assess whether the words we choose are necessary, sincere, and effective. In this chapter, we'll understand how the power of words underlies the success of motivational interviewing.

History and Evolution of Motivational Interviewing

Before we talk about the history and evolution of motivational interviewing, let's understand its definition. Over the years, there have been many versions of this definition, but the one that currently resonates with most practitioners is this: MI is a collaborative method of communication which focuses on—and strengthens—the client's own motivations for change. Through this method, we want an individual to identify and then resolve their own "ambivalence" to change (we'll be discussing this concept in detail soon). There are a few principles that underlie this technique, but let's first understand how this concept came into being and gained popularity over the years.

The field of motivational interviewing owes a lot to William Miller and Stephen Rollnick—two psychologists who have done extensive work on change and addictive behaviors. In 1969, Miller learned about **client-centered psychotherapy**—which contributed to a lot of the principles as well as the "spirit" of motivational interviewing. Some of the important contributions of client-centered psychotherapy to motivational interviewing are:

- having a sense of optimism and acceptance when it came to the belief that the client could find their own solutions to their problems,
- showing empathy through reflective listening, and
- consistently evaluating the effect of our therapeutic style on the clients—thus giving them the power to decide if a certain method or style is working for them.

Another concept that had a huge impact on the development of motivational interviewing is the **self-perception theory** proposed by Daryl Bem. According to Bem, individuals developed a perception about themselves based on their own behaviors, and these behaviors were affected by their social environment and interactions. For example, if a friend thanks me for listening to them, I might perceive myself as a good listener or an empathetic person. Similarly, I might believe that I have an affinity for a certain culture simply because it's what I've been predominantly exposed to for most of my life.

The third major concept that influenced a lot of Miller and Rollnick's work was proposed by Jack Williams Brehm and Sharon Brehm. Known as **reactance theory**, it talks about the need for people to push against change because it is imposed on them. For instance, how many of us have been unable to resist doing something that our parents explicitly forbade us to? How many of us decide to *not* to do something—simply because we've been told that it's good for us? Come to think of it, many of us know what we need to do to improve our lives. Then, what keeps us from taking the required actions? Reactance theory suggests that, unless the need for change comes from within us, we'll resist any ask for change from external agents. Why? Because it threatens our freedom of choice and self-efficacy.

Miller's interest in treating addictive behaviors started in 1972, when he interned under the supervision of Robert Hall at an addiction treatment program. The main focus at this program were alcoholics, who were generally treated using the "controlled drinking" method. He realized that a lot of the clients there didn't find this method helpful. So, he started observing them to better understand how they could be helped.

The interesting thing was, Miller had no real idea about alcoholism, addiction, and the challenges faced by the patients he was observing. However, his lack of "expert knowledge" became an advantage in this case. Since he didn't know anything, he decided to observe these patients and listen to them without judgment and without any intention to change their behaviors. There were two main things that Miller understood about these experiences. One, that most of what he had learned about addiction and addicts—mostly from popular papers written by experts in the field—were negative and discouraging in tone. Miller realized that his own experiences with these people were very different from what he had read so far—maybe because he was allowing them to talk about their experiences as they saw it, which left little room for judgment and erroneous interpretations. The second thing Miller realized was that, by listening to these people without interrupting them, he was able to form a deep and meaningful connection with them.

As Miller started his own teaching and research career, he realized that there was one element that increased the effectiveness of cognitive behavioral therapy (CBT) for treating alcoholism in clients. This element was "therapist empathy." Not only did empathy toward the client make it easier for them to treat their alcoholism in the present, but it also led to more sustained results after a year. In 1983, Miller published a landmark paper called *Motivational Interviewing With Problem Drinkers*, in which he talked about these insights in great detail.

In 1989, Miller met Rollnick and began a partnership that placed motivational interviewing firmly at the center of many therapeutic treatments. The most significant contribution of Rollnick to motivational interviewing was a deep understanding of and respect for "client ambivalence." In most therapeutic practices of that time, the aim was to either ignore or suppress client ambivalence. Simply put, client ambivalence refers to the state in which the client "both wants and doesn't want change." They have enough reasons for wanting to change their behaviors, but they also have reasons to resist change. Instead of assuming that the client is not experiencing ambivalence, Rollnick understood that acknowledging it was the first step toward overcoming it.

Another major departure from most forms of psychotherapy that could be seen in motivational interviewing was the focus on "client language." In other words, Miller and Rollnick believed that if the client could talk about their own motivations for change in a language that they were comfortable with, it could help elicit real change in their behaviors. In 1991, they co-authored a paper called *Motivational Interviewing: Preparing People to Change Addictive Behavior*. Another interesting conclusion they came to was that typically, MI sessions took much less time as compared to both CBT as well as the "12-step program" for alcoholics. Miller and Rollnick suggested that MI-based therapy could be administered in four sessions—two main sessions and two booster sessions at 6 and 12 weeks respectively.

After the publication of their paper, Miller and Rollnick realized that the demand for "qualified" MI trainers had far outstripped their supply. The thing is, neither of them understood the need for certifications and regulations. The reason for this was that they didn't want to spend time focusing on people who were not doing great work in this field. Instead, they wanted to ensure that more and more trainers understood the "spirit" of motivational interviewing. Their focus was on developing excellence rather than regulating mediocrity—which is a revolutionary perspective to have. Their vision gave rise to the first "Training for Teachers" in Albuquerque in 1993, and the "Motivational Interviewing Network of Trainers (MINT)" in 1995. In 2002—almost 20 years after the first paper on MI—the second edition was published, this time with the title *Motivational Interviewing: Preparing People for Change*. This change highlights the fact that motivational interviewing is now used to elicit change in a variety of scenarios. Today, MI can be used as a standalone therapy and also as a companion to other methods such as CBT.

The Core Elements of Motivational Interviewing

In order to understand motivational interviewing in depth, we need to focus on two main aspects of it—its spirit and its principles.

The Spirit of Motivational Interviewing

One of the reasons why Miller and Rollnick were so opposed to "certifications" for trainers was that they saw MI as more than just a set of principles or steps to adhere to. Instead, they wanted trainers to understand and imbibe the spirit of MI in their own work. Without this spirit, their words would have no meaning or impact on the clients. There are three main aspects of the spirit of MI:

- collaboration
- evocation
- autonomy

Another important aspect of the spirit of MI is empathy or compassion.

Let's discuss these elements by taking an example. Imagine that a client has been trying to stick to an exercise regimen for a long time. This person has tried to start an exercise routine multiple times in their life, but they somehow cannot seem to keep going after a while. This is despite the fact that they look good and are complimented by a lot of people as soon as they start looking fitter or more toned. Now, if you're approaching their situation with a traditional therapeutic style, you might rush to provide solutions for them, or judge them for "lacking motivation." You might also try to motivate them by telling them what they should do, or inspire them by comparing them to others. According to MI, these methods won't be able to elicit sustained change in the client, and might even backfire in some cases.

A traditional therapeutic or coaching style might be about confrontation—which means you might try to impose your own perspectives on the client. You might tell them that they're wrong or coerce them into changing their perspectives. This is also because you believe that you're the "expert" and hence, the client needs to listen to you. In a collaborative environment, you and your client together come up with solutions to the problem, and no one's perspective is more important than the other. It's important to note that you don't have to agree with everything your client says, nor does it mean that you don't have more knowledge and expertise than your client in certain areas (especially if you're a medical professional). However, collaborating with your client means that you don't automatically dismiss their opinions and experiences—which is something that many experts tend to do. When we allow our clients to talk about themselves, and listen to them without judgment, we start the crucial process of building faith in our relationship.

Another aspect of a traditional therapeutic style is education. Since the coach believes that they know a lot more than the client, they take it upon themselves to educate the client about their reasons for wanting change. For instance, in this case, you might feel like telling them about the benefits of exercise—even though they might already be aware of them. In some cases, education might come across as condescending. In other cases, it might be a superfluous exercise that doesn't motivate your client to change. In contrast, MI encourages evocation—which means that we talk to our client in such a way that they become aware of their own reasons for change. For example, you might ask the client about their reasons for change, as well as the positive feelings that this change might elicit in their lives.

Your client might tell you that when they exercise regularly, they feel happier or less anxious. They might also like the extra boost of energy they get after exercising. This way, you learn that your client isn't motivated by compliments and appearance-based results, but they certainly enjoy the boost to their mental and emotional health. Now, you can focus on this element of their journey to ensure that they overcome the challenges they're facing in maintaining an exercise routine.

The third aspect of a traditional coaching practice is "authority." If you think of yourself as an expert, you're likely to impose your own rules on your client, directing them to change their behavior as you see fit. In this example, you might prescribe a routine to your client, or set certain rules for them to follow. Through motivational interviewing, however, you can acknowledge your client's autonomy. In other words, you can advise your client and you can work out a plan with them, but you also understand that the ultimate decision lies with them. You respect their choices and give them the power to determine the way ahead. This is not an act of resignation, but an act of placing trust in your partnership.

Principles of Motivational Interviewing

The four main guiding principles of motivational interviewing that were proposed by Miller and Rollnick are:

- **R**esist the righting reflex
- **U**nderstand the patient's own motivations
- **L**isten with empathy
- **E**mpower the patient

Together, they form the acronym RULE. Let's understand these principles in detail.

- **Resist the righting reflex:** The "righting reflex" can be understood as an urge to provide solutions for our clients or patients. This urge comes from the belief that we're the experts and that the client or patient doesn't know anything. Now, I'd like to add a disclaimer here, that this might sometimes be the case. For example, as a nutritionist or a doctor, you're likely to be more aware of what works and what doesn't work for your patient. At the same time, you need to understand that you can only advise the client. It's really up to them to accept or reject your advice, which means that any urge to change should come from within them. The first step toward eliciting lasting change in your client's behaviors is by resisting your own urge to impose your decisions on them. A simple way to do this is by not interrupting your client or patient when they're talking about themselves. This way, you tell them that their own opinions and experiences are equally important during this process.

- **Understand the patient's own motivations:** Once you've taken a step back from dictating your terms to your client, you need to understand what is holding them back from embracing the change they seek in their lives. We come back to the concept of "ambivalence." At this stage, your client might have almost equal reasons for wanting and not wanting to change. When we don't impose our own desires for change on the client, they're prompted to think about the discrepancies between their goals and their current behaviors. When they become aware of *why* they want to change in the first place, they'll also be able to understand why they've not been able to do so till now.

- **Listen with empathy:** In MI, we go beyond simply listening to the patient. In fact, we're able to distinguish between *active listening* and the more passive ways of listening. For example, when your client is telling you something about their challenges, you don't just stay silent or nod along every now and then. For one, you exhibit empathy through your expressions as you listen to the client. At the same time, you're able to ask them questions that help you understand what they're trying to say. We'll discuss more about open-ended questions and reflective listening in the next few chapters.

- **Empower the patient:** Motivational interviewing acknowledges the patient's or client's ability to create the change they want for themselves. When we believe in our client, we make it easier for them to believe in themselves as well. A good MI coach will ensure that their client develops self-efficacy through the process.

Now that we understand the spirit and principles of motivational interviewing, we'll be discussing the core MI skills and techniques in the next few chapters.

Benefits of Motivational Interviewing

Motivational interviewing helps the client in multiple ways, such as:

- It helps the clients see that their coaches have faith in them, thus increasing their own self-confidence in the process.
- It is a great way to build trust and understanding between the client and the coach, thus allowing the client to truly confide in their coach.
- It helps the coaches acknowledge the true barriers to change in a client's life, thus helping in targeted improvement or treatment.
- It helps the client be accountable for their thoughts and behaviors, thus putting them in control of their own narrative.
- By helping coaches understand *why* the client might resist change, MI helps coaches work with the client and make them more receptive to positive change.
- MI is all about supporting the client's self-efficacy, meaning the coaches see them as drivers of change in their own lives.
- By targeting the barriers that make change difficult, MI makes it possible for these changes to be more permanent in nature.

Is MI Really Effective?

As we know, MI originated as a way to help people with a drinking addiction to overcome their urges and stay sober for a longer period of time. With time, MI has proven to be effective in a number of cases, such as

- improving diet patterns,
- helping people overcome problematic behaviors such as smoking, drinking, gambling, and engaging in risky sexual activities,
- reducing and managing weight in a healthy manner,
- managing diabetes symptoms or improving cardiovascular health through lifestyle changes,
- adhering to a treatment and medication plan,

- managing symptoms of chronic pain,
- indulging in regular physical activity to improve health and well-being, and
- supplementing CBT sessions to overcome anxiety disorders and PTSD.

In 2005, a meta-analysis was conducted by researchers to understand how effective MI can be in various scenarios. The results were extremely encouraging. In a statistically significant number of the cases, MI was able to effect positive change in markers of health like blood cholesterol, systolic blood pressure, blood alcohol concentration, and body mass index. Another interesting observation was that MI had an equivalent effect on physiological and psychological diseases. Also, MI has proven itself to be effective in relatively short periods of time. For instance, even as little as 15 minutes of an MI session could bring about a change in the patients in 64% of the cases (Rubak et al., 2005).

In another study, researchers tried to understand whether the use of MI in addition to CBT could help in the treatment of anxiety disorders. The results showed that, in comparison to CBT alone, the combination of MI and CBT was more effective in doing so (Marker & Norton, 2018).

Another interesting aspect of research focuses on adolescent health. On one hand, adolescents are often resistant to change, or they're not taken seriously by many healthcare providers. On the other hand, they are often at a high risk of developing symptoms of anxiety and depression, not to mention eating disorders and addiction disorders. Therefore, it's important to find ways of encouraging adolescents to make use of the help available to them at this time. In one study, it was seen that adolescents who had chronic medical conditions—and were also dealing with anxiety or depression—benefited from MI sessions. They were more receptive to seeking treatment and sticking to the plans laid out for them by their healthcare providers (Reinauer et al., 2018).

Another study showed that when adolescents suffering from anxiety or other mood disorders participated in MI sessions before starting their therapy or medication program, they were more likely to be ready for treatment, and also attended significantly more group therapy sessions than those who had not participated in MI sessions earlier (Dean et al., 2016). These findings help underline the fact that when healthcare providers exhibit empathy toward adolescents—or when they listen to them without condescension or impatience—they support their self-efficacy and allow them to be more enthusiastic about seeking treatment.

Some Things to Consider

Before we examine motivational interviewing on a deeper level, let's discuss some of the challenges that we might face during this practice. For one, it's vital to understand whom these interventions work for. In general, MI is intricately linked to ambivalence, which means that it has a huge impact on those people who *want* to change but aren't able to, for various reasons. In other words, we need the client to meet us halfway in some senses. If the client is absolutely against implementing any change in their lives—or if they're already highly motivated to change—MI interventions might not be able to move the needle, so to speak.

Here are some situations in which MI is particularly helpful:

- **There is low desire and high ambivalence when it comes to making a change in their lives:** Note that there needs to be *some* desire within the client to change, but there is also confusion regarding the need for change. At this stage, the client could go either way, and it is up to the coach to help them resolve their ambivalence.

- **There is some confusion regarding why change is important:** When your client or patient is faced with a treatment plan or a form of therapy, they might resist it simply because they're not certain about the pros and cons of the situation. Here, we need to ensure that we don't just advertise the benefits of a plan. We need to show them any drawbacks or challenges that the plan might have, so that *they* can make an informed decision about it.

- **The client struggles with self-confidence:** MI is really useful in situations where the client often knows what needs to be done in order to improve their condition, but they don't think they have the ability to implement those changes. A good MI coach helps the client believe in themselves, and empowers them to change their lives for the better.

Some of the common barriers that MI coaches and practitioners might encounter are:

- Not being able to dedicate adequate time and effort toward MI training.
- Focusing too much on the "techniques" without understanding and embodying the true spirit of MI.
- Being unable to move away from an "expert" rule when dealing with clients.
- Having to deal with clients who want "quick fixes" instead of lasting change.

Over the years, MI has established itself as an effective and trustworthy intervention method for practitioners across fields. What's more, it can be used to supplement other therapeutic methods and increase their efficacy. In this chapter, we've seen how coaches can benefit immensely from MI training.

The next chapter will help us understand the role that a coach plays in transforming their clients' lives.

Chapter 2
The Role of the Coach

As the world becomes more chaotic, all of us turn to others for guidance, help, or advice. Sometimes, we need the help of those who have more knowledge in a specific domain, or those who have had more years of experience in a particular field. Other times, we simply need someone to listen to us and validate our feelings and experiences. The road to self-discovery and self-improvement can often feel quite lonely, which is why we need others to support and encourage us on our path.

Today, there are numerous coaches, mentors, and teachers in various fields. Even so, not everyone is lucky to have a good coach on their journey. In this chapter, we'll talk about the importance and role of a coach for effective behavior change. We'll also talk about the different qualities that are needed to be a good MI coach, and discuss the ways in which we can learn those qualities.

Who Is a Coach?

Since the term "coach" is bandied about a lot these days, it can be tricky to understand what this role truly stands for. Some of the words that are used interchangeably with "coach" are "mentor," "teacher," and "facilitator." In general, a teacher or a mentor would have very different roles than a coach or a facilitator. While a teacher necessarily needs to teach their students something that they don't previously know, a mentor helps their mentee with advice and guidance. Now, a teacher can act as a mentor in some cases. For example, if a student comes to you with a concern that doesn't directly relate to the subject you're teaching them, you can act as a mentor and help them find their way. Many teachers can also act as "counselors" to their students, especially if they're grappling with career-related concerns.

While a mentor can also step back and let us figure out what we want for ourselves, we usually want to tap into their reserves of knowledge and experience to gain a better perspective of our own path. A facilitator and a coach might also have similarities between them, but generally, these are two separate roles that work in different scenarios. A facilitator is usually helpful when dealing with larger groups. For instance, if a team needs to brainstorm and come up with solutions for a new product, there's a high chance that there will be conflict within the team. Also, the discussion might get derailed every now and then, thus hampering the productivity of the team. During these scenarios, having a facilitator can help by moving the process along, diffusing conflict, and providing everyone with a safe space to express themselves. They help move the discussion along by setting the agenda of the meeting, intervening in case of a conflict, and ensuring the meeting proceeds at a steady pace.

The important thing is, anyone can be a facilitator for a short period of time. For example, you could be a part of the team meeting, but your boss could ask you to act as a facilitator for the meeting. Of course, some scenarios are more complicated than others, so they might need people who are trained in facilitation and moderation. Facilitators can seem involved, but they're focused on order and outcomes of the group, and not necessarily on the needs and aspirations of the individuals.

Now that we know what coaching isn't, let's understand what coaching is. Coaches are different from mentors and teachers not because they don't *have* any useful knowledge or experience, but because they don't flaunt their knowledge when dealing with their clients. An MI coaching relationship is formed when the coach acts like a guide and even a facilitator at some point, but not like an expert.

In general, a coach focuses on one or few very clients at a time. Even if they're coaching in a group, they need to be aware of each individual's desires, challenges, and strengths. While coaches can be subject-matter experts in some cases, they don't always have to be. This is because their aim is to empower their client on their journey, and this can be done simply by asking them open-ended questions and helping them discover their own strengths and weaknesses. In other words, a coach helps the client to learn what they need to, but they don't directly teach them anything. By doing this, a coach can let the client decide for themselves the best ways in which they can achieve their goals.

Traditional Coaching Versus MI Coaching

Traditionally, anyone who took up the role of the coach was supposed to have all the answers. Even today, in many scenarios, a coach is supposed to provide expert advice to their client. However, this is detrimental to the client's progress for multiple reasons. For one, it puts a lot of burden on the coach to make the journey easier for the client. While a coach should ideally make the client feel more confident in themselves, they shouldn't be doing this by providing ready-made solutions to their problems. Not only does this take away from the client's progress, but it also reduces the efficacy of the coach. Similarly, when the coach becomes an expert for the client, the client doesn't need to work on their critical thinking skills, nor do they need to examine their own motivations for change.

You might think that different people work best with different coaching styles, and you would be right. However, if a client is only responding to a directive or prescriptive coaching style, there's a high chance that they'll not be able to effect lasting change in their lives. For example, if I join a gym, I can expect to get a nutrition and exercise plan that I need to follow. Even so, there's no guarantee that I will stick to the plan for a long time. In fact, there's nothing stopping me from giving up on my gym membership and relapsing into old patterns.

Another reason why traditional coaching techniques might not help is that they don't work for people who are already ambivalent about change, and who aren't easily persuaded by "experts" or "fixers." In fact, some people might even get put off by the insistence or even the tone of their coach, and end up doing something entirely different from what they wanted to. Take for instance, a budding sportsperson who is being goaded to perform better by a well-meaning but extremely authoritative coach. This person, if they are extremely resilient, *might* be able to use any negative "motivational" statements made by the coach to their advantage. Many people, however, would ultimately either become demotivated or rebellious—and in both cases, they would have difficulty sustaining any enthusiasm for the sport. This is especially true of teenagers. Since they're already on the fence about so many things, and they usually don't take kindly to authority—it can be very difficult for a coach to help change their behaviors through traditional coaching methods.

An MI coach will understand that their client is the real expert when it comes to their emotions and behaviors. Therefore, a good coach will make it possible for the client to see their own potential—and help them reach that potential—but they will not take on the responsibility of giving advice or solutions in most cases. When solutions are arrived at, it is due to the collaboration between the coach and their client.

In fact, an interesting study was conducted to assess the difference between traditional coaching and MI-based coaching on female teachers who were being encouraged to screen for cervical cancer in Iran. The understanding in cervical cancer research and treatment is that, if women are screened regularly, it is preventable. Even if the cancer is caught early, it's treatable in most cases. However, the challenge lies in getting women to opt for regular screenings, especially after a certain age. In this study, one group of women underwent traditional coaching, while others were exposed to MI-based coaching. After 20 weeks, it was found that only 9% of women who underwent traditional coaching opted for the pap smear (a procedure that tests for cervical cancer in women), compared to almost 21% of women who underwent MI-based coaching (Zolfaghari et al., 2018). As you can see, there's a marked difference between the efficacy of the two methods.

There are some characteristics that any good coach should possess:

- high levels of emotional intelligence (we'll discuss this in greater detail soon)
- good observational skills
- active listening skills
- empathy and compassion
- ability to ask good, open-ended questions
- ability to build a rapport with their clients
- ability to give and receive constructive feedback
- ability to strike a balance between offering support and holding back
- focusing on the client's self-efficacy at all times

We'll be discussing these characteristics in detail in the rest of the chapter.

Building a Collaborative Coaching Relationship

A good coaching relationship needs collaboration at all times. Your client should feel like you are their partner on their journey. Here are some aspects of a collaborative coaching relationship:

- Your client should feel safe in your presence—this includes physical and emotional safety.
- They should be able to come to you without any fear of judgment or unwarranted criticism.
- They should know that their inputs are always welcome, and even encouraged.
- They understand that you're paying attention not only to their outputs, but also to their efforts.
- They feel comfortable communicating with you and being vulnerable in your presence, and vice versa.

A collaborative relationship can only be formed if there's great rapport between you and your client. Some people believe that "rapport" is something that can only be created organically. While it's true that chemistry plays a crucial role in the building of rapport, there's a lot more that goes into it. Let's discuss some of the ways in which you can build rapport with your client as a coach, and lay the foundation for a collaborative relationship:

- **Pay attention to both chemistry and client "coachability":** I've clubbed these points together because they are not in your control as a coach. For one, chemistry is either present in your relationship with the client, or it is not. I'm not implying that your client and you have to be best friends from the get-go, but you both need to be comfortable in each other's presence. If your gut tells you that it might be difficult for you to work with your client, it's much better to give up on the relationship in the beginning. The same goes for coachability. This might seem like a fuzzy term in the beginning, but as you get more experience as a coach, you'll be able to understand whether a client is truly receptive to this relationship or not. For some, it could mean demonstrating the flexibility needed to come up with solutions. For others, it could mean being receptive to—and respectful of—feedback given to them. Here, I'm not talking about ambivalence or resistance to change. Instead, I'm talking about the attitude that your client exhibits as they embark on this journey—being mindful of the challenges they might face on the way, but also being open to a collaborative relationship with you.

- **Check in with your own emotions and reactions:** A coaching relationship is usually an intimate one, which means that it's normal for your emotions to get entangled with that of your client's every so often. However, a good coach is one who can ensure that their own emotions are separate from those of their client's. If your client feels angry or frustrated, you can acknowledge those feelings without getting swept up in them. Similarly, if you get frustrated with the progress made by your client, you can certainly convey them to your client without showing anger or aggression. When we do this, we tell our clients that it's safe for them to open up to us, make mistakes, and even get overwhelmed now and then. We also let them see our ability to balance our coaching responsibilities with our humane side.

- **Keep your ego in check:** This point is related to the previous one, but it deserves a separate discussion. Whether we think of ourselves as the "real experts," or we feel attacked by the client's resistance to change, it can be easy to let our ego lead the way. This might make us appear defensive and even shoot down any valid points that our clients might make. When we let our ego take charge, we risk sacrificing a collaborative relationship for momentary feelings of superiority and triumph. One great way of keeping your ego in check is by asking the client for their opinions as much as you can. You don't have to agree with everything they say, but you'll certainly get comfortable with the idea of entertaining ideas that are not your own (and that might even be opposite to yours).

- **Create a space that makes vulnerability possible:** Vulnerability is often a two-way street. If your client finds you to be the epitome of perfection, they'll be too intimidated to be honest with you about their own struggles. Similarly, if they see you being closed off, they'll wonder whether they're burdening you with their own emotions. Now, there are nuances to this. For instance, in a therapist-patient relationship, a therapist needs to maintain professional boundaries with their patient at all times. They cannot divulge too many details about their own life, while the patient should be able to open up as much as possible. Even in such cases, the patient should be able to see their therapist as human. Even simple statements that help them see you beyond your role as a therapist can help them open up to you.

- **Stay curious about your client at all times:** There are many benefits to curiosity. For example, demonstrating curiosity is an easy way of overcoming judgment. If you feel like you don't understand (or even appreciate) certain behaviors of your client, you can always ask them for more details instead of jumping to the first conclusion that comes to your mind. For example, if your client has difficulty sticking to an exercise regimen, it's easy to assume that they're lazy. Instead, why not ask them about the challenges they face when it comes to exercise? Also, curiosity helps us appreciate the fact that no one exists in a vacuum. The challenges your client faces, or the life they live, don't exist on the outside of the world in which the two of you reside. It's important to understand where your client is coming from, and what is affecting them, to come up with effective solutions to their problems.

Apart from rapport building, there are certain other elements that are a part of a collaborative coaching relationship:

- **Integrity on both sides:** Without integrity, it's impossible to have a healthy coaching relationship with your client. What does integrity mean in this case? Well, for one, you both need to be honest with each other about your strengths and your limitations. It's normal to exaggerate our strengths and downplay our limitations sometimes, but it's not conducive to the relationship. The same goes for any challenges you might face during the coaching journey. The more honest you are with each other, the higher your chances of developing a mutually beneficial relationship.

- **Commitment in terms of time and effort:** Commitment does not imply that you can never encounter dips in motivation or have difficulty sticking to the plan. In fact, being aware of the client's resistance to change is an important aspect of this journey. At the same time, both you and your client should dedicate enough time and effort toward making change possible. Any meaningful collaboration takes time, which means that you should also not be taking on more clients than you can handle at a time.

- **Accountability and trust:** Of course, your client needs to hold themselves accountable for their journey, but so do you. You need to check in with yourself, pay attention to the challenges you're facing as a coach, and take the steps necessary to become better at your role. When you show your client that you can hold yourself accountable, you prompt them to do the same for themselves. Accountability in a relationship is the bedrock of trust and intimacy, because both parties know that the other person takes the relationship—and their role in it—seriously.

Apart from these elements, there are three other elements of a collaborative coaching relationship—empathy and active listening—that we'll discuss in the next few sections.

The Role of Empathy in Coaching

When a client approaches a potential coach, they usually have a specific problem that they need help with. Even if the problem is a bit broad (like, *I want to change my life*), it can be narrowed down into two or three categories. This a position that automatically makes them more vulnerable. For one, they might have to deal with shame regarding their behaviors. If they've been struggling to get over their disordered eating behaviors, for instance, they might already see themselves as weak and unmotivated. In some cases, people they trust—like their parents or teachers—might also look at them as if they don't have enough willpower. As a coach, you're most likely a stranger to them, and one who might have years of experience in this field. This can cause them to feel intimidated. Not only that, but they might also possess the mindset of *No one understands me*. They might even prepare themselves to be misunderstood and treated with condescension.

We already know that patronizing your clients is a complete no-no. At the same time, sympathy might also not be helpful for your clients during this journey. To understand this further, we need to know the difference between "sympathy" and "empathy." While sympathy means that we can commiserate with someone, it doesn't necessarily mean we understand them. We don't identify with their emotions or experiences, but we can show pity or concern for them. While this can be helpful in some cases, it is often counterproductive with clients who are resistant to change. When your client realizes that you don't really understand their struggles, they might find it difficult to open up to you.

So, what does empathy mean in a coaching relationship? When we exhibit empathy toward another, we are able to truly appreciate their perspective. Now, you might think, how can I possibly empathize with— as a man—the experiences of a woman? This is where the difference between emotional and cognitive empathy comes in. While emotional empathy means that we *feel* the exact (or almost similar) emotions as another, cognitive empathy implies that we *understand* or *appreciate* their emotions because we've learned how they might feel in a particular instance. For example, a woman who has experienced the challenges of pregnancy and childbirth firsthand will find it easy to exhibit emotional empathy toward someone having a similar experience. However, a woman who hasn't gone through this process—or even a man—can read up about the many obstacles that someone in this situation might face. They can listen to interviews, talk to other people who have gone through similar experiences, and inform themselves as much as they can about these issues. When they do this, they'll be able to exhibit cognitive empathy toward them.

Apart from appreciating another person's perspective, empathy asks us to reserve judgment on them, and being able to sit in the feelings that arise. It's true that some people are more empathetic than others, but it's equally true that empathy is like a muscle that can be exercised. Here are a few simple ways in which you can practice more empathy toward your clients:

- **Make sure you're using language that your client is comfortable with:** This might seem like a small thing, but remember that we want our clients to feel less intimidated and more comfortable with us. They shouldn't feel like we're the expert and they know nothing, and this is a signal that can be sent when we start using jargon. Now, this language might be extremely common among our peers, but our client is not one of them. So, keep in mind that you should always communicate in clear and simple language, without talking down to the client. This is important. If your client feels like you're "dumbing down" concepts for them, they might feel humiliated and alienate themselves from you.

- **When in doubt, ask:** We come back to the concept of making your client a partner on this journey. Don't start with the assumption that you have to know everything. The more open-ended and respectful questions you ask your client, the easier it will be for you to understand them. You can start with really broad questions, and slowly narrow down to questions that are pertinent to their particular situations. At all times, allow for the possibility of being wrong. Taking accountability for your own mistakes can make them see you as human, and become more vulnerable with you.

- **Get comfortable with uncomfortable feelings:** One of the reasons why empathy can be so difficult to put into practice is due to the feelings that surface when we practice it. For example, if you're listening to someone talk about their difficult childhood, it can trigger your own memories and emotions related to similar experiences. Even if you've not gone through something similar, it can be uncomfortable to face such intense emotions from another person. Therefore, practicing ways to "sit" in these feelings is an important tool that can help us stay empathetic without feeling overwhelmed. One of the best ways to do this is through mindfulness, which is something we'll be exploring in a future chapter.

The Importance of Active Listening in Coaching

Active listening is an important aspect of empathy, which is why it's also known as "empathetic listening." It might seem a bit weird to differentiate between passive and active listening, as all kinds of listening should ideally center on the speaker. The truth is, many of us are ill-equipped for active listening. In a world where everyone is clamoring for attention—and where there's an avalanche of information coming our way at any given time—many of us barely listen to the other person. Even if we do, we're usually so preoccupied with our own concerns that we forget to truly pay attention to what the other person is trying to tell us.

There are other ways in which we might not be empathetic listeners. In some cases, we might think of ourselves as an expert—which means that we might interrupt our speakers or dismiss their concerns. Sometimes, we might not even be aware that we're behaving in this manner. In other cases, we might listen to them attentively but struggle to withhold judgment in the process. Therefore, even if we're listening to them, we're undermining what they have to say through our expressions or mannerisms.

Here are some questions you can ask yourself to judge whether you're an active listener or not:

- Do I usually talk more than I listen during an average conversation?
- Do I tune out or get distracted too soon or too often when someone else is talking?
- Do I choose who to listen to, and who to ignore (through unconscious biases)?
- Do I have a difficult time listening to someone who has an opposing view to mine?
- Do I dislike being challenged or questioned?
- Do I have trouble concentrating on someone who isn't exactly an eloquent speaker, or whose mannerisms put me off?
- Do I have a habit of dismissing other people's views or emotions, or do I keep persuading others to not feel or think a certain way?
- Am I always quick to give advice or suggestions, without even asking if the other party wants it?
- Do I listen only to speak again, or am I always waiting for my chance to speak—even when someone else is talking?

If you've answered yes to most of these, you might need to work on your active listening skills. Before we discuss these skills, let's understand how active listening can help us strengthen our relationship with our clients. For one, it helps us pick up on cues that we might otherwise miss out on. For instance, our client might be unwilling to tell us something about themselves, but we can notice that they get uncomfortable or anxious when discussing certain topics—which can give us clues regarding the challenges they face in their lives. Active listening helps us make the best use of both verbal and nonverbal cues to gain a deeper understanding of the situation.

Active listening also helps us gain our client's trust because it shows them that we're interested in what they have to say. It shows them that we respect their feelings and opinions, and that we truly want to work with them to overcome their challenges. Like most of MI, active listening can sometimes—ironically—feel "passive" in its approach. After all, we're not really engaging in conventional conversation with our client at this time. However, it is this act of stepping back and letting them express themselves that can encourage our clients to take action. When they feel truly heard, they automatically gain more confidence in themselves, and are encouraged to come up with solutions in partnership with you.

Here are some tips that can help you develop your active listening skills as a coach:

- **Pay undivided attention to your client:** No matter how busy you are, the time you spend with your client is sacred. Unless there's an emergency, you should not be on your phone or checking your mail when your client is talking to you. Just as you're tuned in to their body language at this time, they are too. So, ensure that you convey respect, curiosity, and empathy at all times. If you have trouble focusing on your client, you can use this opportunity to make small notes for you to remember later. Don't overdo this, however, and try to maintain gentle eye contact with your client as much as possible.

- **Understand where your client is coming from:** If you're prone to showing judgment, practice empathy and try to understand your client's context. A simple way of doing this is by being aware of any cultural, linguistic, economic, social, educational, or other identity-based differences between the two of you. Not only will this help you exhibit empathy during your sessions, but it will also keep you from making any tone-deaf suggestions in the future.

- **Reflect on their feelings and opinions:** An important thing to understand here is that you don't have to agree with everything your client says or believes in. Active listening is not the same as being your client's "yes man." When we reflect on their feelings, however, we take ourselves out of the equation and ask them if we're able to understand them accurately. For example, if your client says that they simply cannot lose weight through home-cooked meals, you don't have to agree with them. You can, instead, ask them why they feel this way and what their own experiences have been regarding home-cooked food. Asking open-ended questions in a non-combative manner can go a long way in making your client feel heard and respected.

- **Paraphrase what your client tells you:** When you effectively paraphrase your client's statements, you show them that you've been listening attentively to them. At the same time, you don't want to mindlessly parrot what they've said, as it can come across as condescending. What you want to do is choose the main points that stood out to you from their statements, and ask them if you've indeed understood the situation properly. For instance, in the example of home-cooked food and weight loss, your client might come from a family and culture where it's difficult to follow a healthy diet. Their food might be rich in carbohydrates and saturated fats, and not enough on proteins or green vegetables. You don't want to dismiss their culture or ask them to make drastic changes to their diet, but you can make them see that you appreciate the unique challenges they face on this journey. This can prompt them to come up with solutions, and also establish you as a trustworthy person in their lives.

- **Exchange feedback with your client:** Feedback is a tricky thing to implement in your coaching relationship, and we'll discuss this in some detail in the future. When it comes to feedback, ask your client if they're willing to receive it after your active listening session. It shouldn't feel to them that you're more focused on giving feedback than on understanding them. Similarly, when you feel ready, ask your client to provide feedback regarding your listening skills. Like any other skill, we become better at active listening through regular practice and feedback.

In this chapter, we've discussed how to form a collaborative relationship with our clients through rapport building, empathy, and active listening. In the next chapter, we'll be taking a deep dive into various motivational interviewing strategies.

Chapter 3
Techniques for Effective Motivational Interviewing

Since motivational interviewing is a dynamic field—and one that can be applied to various scenarios—practitioners are always coming up with techniques that can help the clients evoke change in their lives. That being said, there are a few basic techniques that are essential for anyone who wants to train as an MI coach. Think of these techniques as gears in a well-oiled machine. When each of these gears is in place, the machine functions well. Together, they might make the MI process seem effortless and intuitive, but if even one of these gears is missing—or not working properly—the entire machinery grinds to a halt.

As you become more confident in your coaching journey, you'll likely start to make connections between these techniques, and come up with certain practices of your own. For now, this chapter will help you become confident in these essential MI techniques. Additionally, we'll also take a deep dive into the concepts of "ambivalence," "change talk," and client motivations.

Core Motivational Interviewing Techniques

The four core techniques or skills used in MI are

- Open-ended questions,
- Affirmations,
- Reflections (or Reflective Listening), and
- Summaries.

Together, they are known as OARS. In this section, we'll talk about mastering open-ended questions, affirmations, and summaries.

Open-Ended Questions to Arrive at Insights

Open-ended questions are also known as exploratory questions. These are questions that cannot be answered with a simple "yes" or "no." The aim of asking these questions is to better understand your client's motivations for change, and to come up with creative solutions based on the insights gained from them. A close-ended question is limiting in nature, especially when you want your client to dig deep into their own story and examine their reasons for—and resistance to—change. These questions allow your client to assume full control over the conversation, and they might even take them to surprising places on their journey of self-discovery. Generally, these questions start with "What," "Why," or "How." However, there's more to the art of asking effective open-ended questions. Let's discuss a few of these points below:

- **These questions need to be asked in a curious and respectful manner:** When we ask open-ended questions, we don't start with assumptions about our client. For example, if your client tells you that they struggle to get up in the morning, you should not ask, "What do you think causes you to be *lazy* in the morning?" This might *sound* like an open-ended question, but there's already a sense that you know at least part of the answer to it. Instead, you can ask, "What are the challenges you face when trying to get up early?"

- **Make sure that your questions are free of judgment:** As coaches, we try really hard to not let our clients feel judged, but it's also crucial to understand that many of our clients might be sensitive when discussing aspects of their lives.

During this exchange, we need to make sure that we don't put them on the spot. While we want to elicit responses from them, they should feel comfortable exploring their deepest emotions in our presence. For example, if your client tells you that they have issues with impulse control when it comes to their food choices, they're already feeling vulnerable and being hard on themselves. At this time, even a simple question like "Why can't you control your impulses?" can seem pointed and accusatory to them—leading them to get defensive or feel worse about themselves. Instead, you can frame your question more kindly, such as, "What do you think makes it difficult for you to control your impulses, even though you really want to?" The essence of the question remains the same, but this small change will put your client at ease.

- **Use open-ended questions to explore your client's feelings and opinions, and take the focus away from their behaviors:** An interesting technique of asking open-ended questions can help us gain deeper insights into our client's behaviors, without making them feel targeted in the process. For example, let's say your client tells you that they have been struggling to eat healthy for a while now. Instead of asking them questions regarding this behavior of theirs—such as, "Why do you fail to stick to your diet plan?" or "What are the challenges you face when trying to eat healthy?" why not ask them about the feelings around these challenges and experiences? For instance, you can ask them, "How does this make you feel?" or "What are the thoughts that cross your mind during this time?" It might seem like a simple change, but focusing on our client's feelings instead of their behaviors can often help us connect to them on a deeper level. They might not realize it, but they'll be able to uncover their true motivations for change. For instance, if your client realizes that they are wary of how unhealthy eating can affect their energy levels throughout the day, they'll understand why it's so important for them to stick to their diet plan.

Some examples of open-ended questions are:
- How can I support you on this journey?
- How can I make you feel safer or validated as your coach?
- What is it that you're looking for through this program?
- How has your [insert goal] journey been so far?
- Can you tell me more about that?
- Why don't we spend some time exploring these emotions?
- What else would you like to explore with me?

As you can see, there's no dearth of open-ended questions you can ask your client—especially as you get to know them better. Often, a good question will elicit responses that you can use to ask more open-ended questions. The important thing is to give your client the time they need to explore these questions, and to stay with a question until you reach an insight about them.

Affirmations to Support Your Client's Self-Efficacy

We've discussed a little bit about the concept of self-efficacy in the previous chapters. This concept was introduced by psychologist Albert Bandura as part of his Social Cognitive Theory—which talks about how people adapt to and master their environment. In other words, it helps us find a connection between our cognition, behavior, and environment. Essentially, self-efficacy means the belief that we have in our talents and efforts, or the confidence that we can achieve mastery in whatever activity we take up.

People with high self-efficacy are usually more committed to their goals and activities, have high resilience—meaning they can bounce back from setbacks and failures—and focus on achieving mastery in their skills. In other words, challenges don't scare them; instead, they are seen as opportunities for growth. As you can imagine, this mindset is really conducive to creating lasting change in our lives. In fact, high self-efficacy is related closely to the "growth mindset," while low self-efficacy is usually connected to the "fixed mindset." Someone with a fixed mindset will likely believe that they cannot change their behaviors, or that setbacks are an indication of failure. Such people are less likely to "dust themselves off" and begin again after having fallen down.

We should also understand the difference between self-confidence and self-efficacy. While self-confidence is more about how we think about ourselves in general, self-efficacy can vary according to the scenario. For example, I might have complete belief in my abilities when it comes to work, but I might not believe enough in my ability to take care of myself. Similarly, I might have high self-efficacy when it comes to following an exercise routine, but low self-efficacy in terms of healthy eating.

Now that we know what self-efficacy is, and how it can pave the way for lasting change, let's talk about the ways in which we can develop high self-efficacy, and what that means for you as a coach:

- **Our moods, stress levels, and reactions to various situations:** When we're feeling stressed or tired, we might have lower self-efficacy than usual. At the same time, if we can reframe these moods in a positive manner, we can improve our self-efficacy. What does this mean for you as a coach? Of course, you need to check in with your client and understand what's going on in their lives currently—especially if they seem dejected or unmotivated about doing what needs to be done.

- **Our experience of mastering a skill or achieving success in something:** When we achieve some form of success—no matter how small—our self-efficacy increases. We can use the high that comes with this achievement to pursue other, harder goals. Interestingly, the task that we achieve mastery in needs to be doable, but just a little difficult. If it's too easy, the win won't mean much to us. As a coach, what you can do is come up with a plan where your client tries to do one thing that is difficult but not impossible for them.

- **Persuasion from others in the form of affirmations and encouragement:** When we have someone who truly believes in us, it makes it easier for us to believe in ourselves. Of course, this person should be someone we trust and respect. As a coach, you're in a powerful position to influence your client's attitudes and behaviors.

How Can Affirmations Help?

Affirmations are positive statements that make us believe in our strengths and abilities. Self-affirmations can help your client overcome their negative thinking patterns and gain self-efficacy, but they might be difficult to implement in the beginning of their journey. As their coach, you can use affirmations to help your clients overcome any feelings of doubt or negativity. You can also help them focus on their strengths and on their progress rather than the outcomes—especially if those outcomes are less than optimal right now. What's more, when you use affirmations to motivate your client, you also model a healthy behavior for them to emulate when they are on their own.

While affirmations should always be positive, they should also be realistic and consistent. If you cannot provide evidence that supports your affirmation, your client might feel cheated on or patronized by you. For example, if your client hasn't been exercising at their regular level for a week or so, they're likely to be disappointed in themselves. At this time, you cannot say something like, "I'm glad you've been pushing yourself hard" because it's simply not true. Rather, you can say "I'm so proud of you for having showed up every day of the week, even though you would like to perform better." This tells your client that you're aware of their challenges as well as their efforts.

Similarly, you should always gradually build on your affirmations, especially if your client is being too hard on themselves. For instance, if your client is feeling angry or stressed, they might get irritated when you exude too much positivity around them. Instead, you can simply acknowledge the fact that they're trying to work on themselves during this time. Sometimes, it takes time for us to believe the good things we hear about ourselves, especially if we've been in a negative spiral for a long time. Allow your client to get used to your affirmations and positive talk.

Here are a few examples of healthy affirmations you can use:

- I'm so glad that you've come to me for guidance and support.
- I appreciate you choosing to be vulnerable with me.
- I can see that you're a very resilient person.

- You have the ability to handle yourself well in demanding situations.
- I can see that you've been working hard to overcome the challenges we talked about.

Remember to be as specific as possible about the behavior or attitude that you're affirming, as it increases your client's faith in you.

Summaries to Help Gain Deeper Understanding of Your Client

In the previous chapter, we had a section on active listening as a tool to collaborate with—and understand—your client. Open-ended questions, affirmations, reflective listening, summarization, and paraphrasing are all tools from the "active listening" toolkit. When we've listened carefully to our client, we can summarize the main points of the discussion, identify its key themes, and also let them know if we want more clarification on certain points. Summaries should be accurate and succinct, and they should tell us everything we need to remember about the discussion. You can summarize at the end of a conversation, or you can decide to do so at regular intervals. What is important here is the difference between summaries, reflection, and paraphrasing.

Summarization usually means that we keep the content and language as intact as possible. We don't want to introduce our own interpretations here. Thus, summaries can help indicate the end of a session, and they can also bring structure to a meandering discussion. Also, when our clients "hear back" their own thoughts, they often gain a new perspective in the process. Hence, good summaries can help you and your client make a plan for future sessions as well.

Paraphrasing, on the other hand, can include some of your own perspectives as well. Be mindful to not impose your own views on your client when you paraphrase your discussion with them. Instead, let them know that there are certain interpretations you've made of this discussion, and ask them about their views on the same. One good way of summarizing or paraphrasing is to start with "What I understand is..."

Reflection can happen multiple times during a conversation, and it simply means that we "hold a mirror" to our client's thoughts and feelings. We can use reflection to help our client talk more about themselves or their issues, or to help them expand on a topic during the conversation. Your summary can also be the sum total (in a sense) of your reflections throughout the conversation. Please ensure that you reflect not only the words, but also the feelings of your client during a conversation with them. This can only happen when we practice empathy during our interactions with the client.

Now that we've familiarized ourselves with the techniques we can use for motivational interviewing, let's talk about understanding our client's motivations, handling their ambivalence, and evoking "change talk" to help them reach their goals.

Unpacking Client Motivations

In order to ensure lasting change in our client's lives, we need to understand their true motivations for pursuing it in the first place. The best way to understand why your client wants to change something is by asking them open-ended questions about their decisions. For instance, you can ask them "Why do you want this change in your life?" or "What do you think will happen once you make this change in your lifestyle?" Give them time to talk about their goals, challenges, and aspirations in detail.

Let's first understand the different kinds of motivation that exist:

- **Complete lack of motivation:** As we've discussed before, coaches usually don't work with someone who has no motivation at all for change. At the very least, we need our clients to experience a little bit of ambivalence.

- **Extrinsic motivation:** This kind of motivation originates outside of ourselves. In some cases, people might come to you because they've been asked to change by those close to them. For instance, someone might join a fitness program on the insistence of their spouse. Other times, people want change, but for superficial reasons—such as, they want to be complimented by others for having lost weight. The problem with extrinsic motivation is that it depends on external circumstances, which means that it can fizzle out at any given moment. What happens, for instance, if someone works really hard and loses a lot of weight, but they don't get the validation they were looking for?

- **Intrinsic motivation:** When a client is intrinsically motivated, they have valid reasons for wanting to change, and these reasons are dependent on what they want for themselves. Such people will usually have little to no issues with changing their behaviors. Coaches can certainly work with them, but they usually adopt a facilitator-type role in these cases.

- **Introjected motivation:** This kind of motivation is usually impacted by negative feelings toward oneself. For example, if I feel ashamed that I have put on a lot of weight, I might want to join a fitness program. Or, I might feel guilty for letting myself go during the holiday season, and vow to start eating healthy in the new year. These feelings can certainly keep us motivated for a while, but good coaches don't rely on them for lasting change. In fact, they recognize that clients who understand the positive impact of change on their lives will be the ones to stick with the change for a longer period of time.

- **Identification and integration:** Think of it as acknowledging client ambivalence, and appreciating the value of coaching in resolving it. We want our clients to be able to explore their own reasons for—and resistance toward—change.

You can even look at these types as stages of motivation. For instance, someone who once experienced introjected or extrinsic motivation can finally reach a state of ambivalence on their journey. We identify our client's motivations by asking them open-ended questions, but we want to make sure that we're uncovering their deeper motivations instead of the superficial ones. For instance, your client might tell you that they want to lose a certain amount of weight in the next few months because they want to look good. However, chances are that this surface-level motivation is tied to something unique about them. Why is it important for them to look good, for example? Who do they want to look good for? Is "looking good" related to receiving better opportunities in some way? Or, is it about being able to accept themselves? Maybe "looking good" will make them feel confident about attending social events and feeling less isolated in their lives. Until you're able to understand their core motivations, you won't be able to help them achieve meaningful change in their lives.

Identifying and Handling Client Ambivalence

Many people who approach coaches for improving a certain aspect of their lives are in a state of ambivalence regarding their journey of change. Ambivalence is not the same as "neutrality." When we're neutral about a certain behavior or goal, we don't have positive or negative feelings about it. For instance, I might acknowledge the benefits and challenges of healthy eating, but I don't have a personal opinion on it and am not moved by these points in any way. On the other hand, if I appreciate how great I feel after a week of healthy eating, but I also know that it's hard for me to resist eating ultraprocessed food, I'm experiencing a state of ambivalence. On one hand, I want nothing more than to experience the benefits that come with this change. On the other, I find it extremely difficult to stick to this change. Remember that ambivalence exists *within* an individual, meaning a coach helps the client identify their own ambivalence, rather than listing the pros and cons of a decision for them.

Also, they don't dismiss the feelings that arise during this process. For instance, if the client tells the coach that they are intimidated by the thought of weekly meal prepping, the coach does not say, "Oh, that's very easy, and lots of people do it. You're worried about nothing." Clearly, the client is worried enough for them to be unsure of embracing this change.

There are three main kinds of ambivalence to look out for:

- **Affective ambivalence:** This is a state of having conflicting *feelings* about something. For example, if I want to change my career after 10 years in the same field, I will likely feel excited about learning and trying my hand at something new. At the same time, I might feel scared and worried about venturing into the unknown.

- **Cognitive ambivalence:** In this state, we have conflicting *thoughts* about a particular decision. For instance, I might think that a career change will give me more exposure to different industries, but I might also worry about the hours of time and effort I would have to put into learning something from scratch. Here, I'm experiencing ambivalence regarding the same decision, but I'm not approaching it from an emotional angle.

- **Affective-cognitive ambivalence:** In this state, we have a classic "head versus heart" conflict. For example, my heart tells me to take a leap into the unknown and chase my passion, while my mind tells me to consider the financial and practical implications of such a decision.

Why is it important to recognize the type of ambivalence your client is dealing with? When we know what is fueling the conflict within them, we can help them address the conflict effectively. For example, if my client is faced with a "head versus heart" decision, I might need to probe further into both the practical and emotional aspects of their lives. As I discuss their motivations for change, I might realize that their biggest fear isn't financial loss, but having to live with regret for the rest of their lives. Once I identify the strongest motivator for change, I can help them make decisions that support their core motivations.

The Stages-of-Change Model

Once we've identified the ambivalence within our client, we need to help them embrace change on their journey. The "Stages-of-Change" model is a very helpful framework developed by James Prochaska and Carlo DiClemente in 1983, to help addiction therapists understand the progression of a patient's attitude toward change (Shaffer, 2013). Following are the steps outlined in the model, as well as the actions that a coach (or a therapist, in their case) should take to help the client or patient willingly change their behaviors:

Stage 1: Precontemplation

At this stage, the client is not ready for change. So, it might be useful for the coach to explain to them the risks associated with maintaining the "status quo." As a coach, you might choose to not work with someone who is at least a little ambivalent about change, but a therapist or doctor often does not have that luxury. In that case, they might need to highlight the health risks associated with following a certain lifestyle. As you can see, we want to bring the patient to a state of introjected motivation, where negative emotions like guilt and fear prompt them to take the next step.

Stage 2: Contemplation

This is a state of ambivalence, and this is where most coaches start from. Here, we want the client to identify the pros and cons of the decisions they're trying to make. We want to explore the reasons for their ambivalence, and help them realize the discrepancies between their core motivations and their current behaviors. Also, this is the stage where we support our client's self-efficacy, so that they can confidently move toward the change they desire in their lives.

Stage 3: Preparation and Action

Now that our client has decided to change their behaviors, we need to help them with setting goals and preparing an action plan to achieve these goals.

Stage 4: Maintenance

For many people, the most challenging part of the change process is the maintenance stage. At this point, they don't want to lose the progress they've made on their change journey. So, the coach works with the client to identify ways in which a relapse can be prevented.

Stage 5: Relapse (also known as the "Learning" stage)

What happens when your client relapses into past behavior patterns? Understandably, they might feel demoralized and even disappointed in themselves. This is, therefore, a crucial stage because it can determine whether your client will bounce back from this setback or give up on their journey. In MI, relapse is not seen as a failure but a normal part of the change process. In fact, the success of the program usually depends on how well the client can respond to a setback, and how they can use it as an opportunity to build resilience. If this stage is handled well, it can help the client form and stick to lifelong habits.

Evoking Change Talk

One of the main aspects of the spirit of MI is evocation. We want our client to embrace change on their own, which is why we want them to resolve their ambivalence not because we're confronting them, but because they can understand the importance and benefits of change in their lives. According to Miller and Rollnick, there are three main components of motivation in a client—willingness, ability, and readiness. The client should acknowledge the importance of change for themselves, and therefore, be willing to change. They should also believe that this change is a priority for them, which makes them ready to embrace it. Last but not least, they should also believe that they have what it takes to create change in their lives.

If you as a coach keep advocating for change—no matter how compelling your arguments are—your client will likely become defensive against it. Therefore, we need the client to find and articulate their own reasons for change—which then becomes a part of their "change talk." An ambivalent client will usually have two kinds of statements running through their minds at any time. Statements that support change (known as change talk) will sound something like these:

- *I am ready to change my routine.*
- *I want to eat healthier so that I feel more active during the day.*
- *I'm worried about the consequences of not changing my habits.*

Statements that support maintenance of status quo (known as sustain talk) sound these like the following:

- *I've tried so many times and failed; I don't think it's possible for me to change.*
- *I'm used to how things are; I don't think there's a real need for me to change.*
- *I'm worried about the amount of time and effort I'll have to put in to make this change possible.*

As a coach who wants their client to change, it can be tempting to only focus on your client's "change talk," but you need to also pay close attention to—and acknowledge—their "sustain talk." This way, you'll be able to understand what truly stands in their way. Active listening plays a very crucial role during this process, as you need to focus not only on what your client's telling you, but also on their body language, tone, and other nonverbal expressions.

Here are a few methods you can use to elicit change talk from your client:

- **Use open-ended questions to evoke answers supporting change:** Ask your clients questions about their current routines, goals, and challenges. Try to understand why it's important for them to pursue change. For instance, you can ask them, "Why do you want to lose weight, and why is it important to do so now?" Remember, you need to give your client time and space to work through their response. You can also ask them *how* important it is for them to change at that point in time, so that you can assess how ready they are for the process.

- **Talk about the pros and cons of the decision they're considering:** Your client probably already has a pros and cons list in their mind, but you need to explore them in great detail during your conversation with them. Let's take an example of this. If you ask your client to talk about the advantages of regular exercise, they might say something like "I feel fit and active when I exercise regularly, and I'm able to spend more time playing with my grandchildren." When you ask them why they're not able to commit to a schedule, they might say "I'm extremely busy throughout the day." As they begin articulating these pros and cons, they might arrive at two insights. One, that they might be able to include their kids in some of their exercises or physical activities. And two, that regular exercise helps them make the most of the time they do get to spend with their grandkids. So, dedicating some time to their exercise regimen can help improve the quality of free time they get during the day.

- **Ask them to elaborate on their reasons for and against change:** The more involved your client is in understanding their own motivations for and against change, the better they'll get at recognizing the discrepancies in their behaviors.

- **Use summaries and reflective listening to your advantage:** Motivational interviewing practitioners believe that our client already has everything they need to push for change within themselves. All we need to do is to make them see those reasons for themselves, and effective summarization and reflective listening can help us do this.

- **Explore your client's deepest fears and desires:** This needs to be done with care, as we don't want our clients to get triggered or scared of the process. Done well, it might help them understand the worst and best case scenarios of both changing and not changing. If your client understands that the cost of maintaining the status quo is much higher than making a change, they might be motivated to take the plunge.

- **Talk in terms of goals and lessons:** When clients don't want to change, they're often stuck in the past, thinking about their "failures." Instead, talk to them about any wins they might have had, and how those wins made them feel. For instance, ask your client to tell you about a stretch of time when they were able to maintain a healthy diet. How did they feel at this time? Would they want to feel the same way again? You can also talk to them about future goals, and how those goals would improve their life. Give them a chance to either remember or visualize their "changed" life.

Now that we've discussed in detail the various motivational interviewing techniques that can help our clients move toward lasting change, let's apply these techniques in various fields. In the next chapter, we'll discuss the use of MI in fitness coaching.

Chapter 4
Motivational Interviewing in Fitness and Exercise

Years of research has shown us the many benefits of regular physical exercise. Even 30 minutes of exercise each day can vastly improve our physical and mental health. Having said that, many people struggle to make exercise a part of their daily lives. In fact, research shows that less than 5% of adults exercise for 30 minutes each day (*Exercise & Fitness: Facts & Statistics*, n.d.)! What does this mean for us as coaches? For one, it's clear that there's a huge gap between intention and behavior for most people. Also, many of the current "motivational" programs aren't really working for them. Most importantly, however, it means that MI-based coaches can make a real difference in the lives of people who envision a healthier life for themselves.

Boosting Self-Efficacy for Building a Lifelong Practice

In the last chapter, we talked about how important self-efficacy is for clients who want lasting change in any aspect of their lives. Turns out, having high self-efficacy is extremely important for "exercise adherence." Exercise adherence is a term that refers to a person's ability to stick to an exercise routine on a consistent basis, especially in the face of (actual or perceived) barriers. Let's discuss some of the ways in which we can help our clients boost their self-efficacy regarding regular exercise.

Encourage Your Client to Engage in Positive Self-Talk

Positive self-talk is a great way for our clients to overcome any negative beliefs they might have about themselves. Many of these negative thoughts can come to the surface when our client engages in "sustain talk." For instance, if your client believes that a certain exercise routine is too hard for them, they can tell themselves that they don't need to master the routine in one day. They can say something like, *If I keep at it regularly, it'll get less hard each day*. Your client doesn't need to engage in toxic positivity, or to ignore the very real challenges they might be facing on their journey. All they need to do is reframe any self-limiting beliefs into more rational and encouraging ones.

Help Your Client See Exercise in a Positive Light

If your client thinks of exercise as boring, difficult, or punitive in nature, it can be very challenging for them to stick to a routine. If they're already feeling defeated or fatigued when they think of exercise, it's highly unlikely that they will experience high self-efficacy around it. Therefore, work with your client to reframe how they view exercise. For one, you can help them shift the focus on the feelings they have during and after the session rather than those they have just before. This is because physical exercise releases feel-good hormones like dopamine, serotonin, and oxytocin. All of these can improve your client's mood as well as their perceptions of exercise.

For instance, I have days when I simply don't feel like leaving the bed to take a walk. However, I've found that if I can drag myself to a park nearby and walk for even 15 minutes, I start feeling better almost immediately. The challenge, then, is to remember this feeling when I'm ambivalent about going for my daily walk. How do I achieve this? By recording myself when I'm experiencing a "high" during and after my walk. In this recording, I talk about how happy I am that I decided to go for a walk and how good I feel after only 15 minutes of walking. Then, when I am in two minds about sticking to my walking routine, I play back this recording to myself, and it has a positive impact on me more often than not!

Another thing you can do is work with your client to find something that they truly enjoy doing. While they might need to do a variety of exercises to achieve different fitness goals, they should be able to enjoy a major portion of their routine. For instance, if a client enjoys dancing, you should work with them to make that a part of their routine. If they feel more motivated while exercising in a group, ensure that they're able to participate in more group activities. If your client is frequently stressed or bored when exercising, it'll be very difficult for them to build the self-efficacy needed to keep at it.

Set Realistic Goals and Milestones With Your Clients

Nothing will convince your client that they can achieve their goals more than the progress they see on their journey. For this, it's extremely important that you help them set specific, measurable, achievable, realistic, and time-bound (SMART) goals. For instance, if your client's goal is "losing weight in the next few months," they'll likely find it difficult to stay motivated throughout their journey. Instead, if they have a goal like, "I want to lose 15 pounds in the next 6 months in a healthy and sustainable manner," they'll not only be more focused and motivated, but they'll also be able to steadily track their progress and celebrate their wins through manageable milestones.

An ideal goal is one that doesn't intimidate your client, and yet, urges them to step a little out of their comfort zone. Make sure that they spend some time determining their goals and milestones, because you want them to be invested in their own journey. They shouldn't feel like these goals have been imposed on them. When it comes to tracking these goals and milestones, ask your client what works best for them. Are they comfortable with digital apps and fitness trackers? How often do they want to measure or weigh themselves? How do they respond to the changes they see in themselves?

One great way for your client to keep track of their progress and find motivation within themselves is by keeping an "exercise journal." In this journal, they can record how often they exercise, and for how long. They can also note down their thoughts and feelings before and after the exercise sessions. Over time, this record can help them choose the best period during the day for exercise, and also help them remember how exercise helps them—especially on days they're not feeling up to it.

Build Your Client's Confidence Using Past Experiences

In the last chapter, we talked about how mastering a skill can boost our self-efficacy. In simple terms, when we look back and think, *I was able to overcome these obstacles and master this exercise*, it's much easier for us to believe that we can repeat our success in the present and future. As a coach, what you can do is record your client's achievements, so that you can play them back to your client when they need motivation. At the same time, you can use these "mastery" experiences to learn more about your client, their motivations, and their behaviors. Using these experiences, you can also help your client set goals that challenge them a little. For instance, if they previously thought that they couldn't walk for more than 15 minutes at a stretch—but are now able to walk 20 minutes in one go—you can help them set a goal of walking 30 minutes without stopping. Of course, you need to ensure that these goals are challenging but not too difficult to achieve, as you want your client to stay motivated throughout the process.

Use the Power of Visualization to Build Your Client's Self-Efficacy

If your client has achieved a similar goal of theirs in the past, it becomes a bit easier to motivate them in the present. If this is not the case, or if they're a beginner, you can help them visualize future successes in order to build their self-efficacy. Visualization is also a great tool for enhancing their focus and challenging themselves. What makes visualization such a powerful technique? Studies have shown that visualization has the same effect on the brain as actual "physical practice." For instance, when we visualize ourselves as doing a certain exercise, the areas of our brain that are affected by this exercise light up in the same way as when we're actually doing the exercise.

According to research done at Cleveland Clinic Foundation in Ohio, people who went to the gym recorded a 30% increase in their muscle strength, while those who simply visualized the workouts showed a 13.5 increase (*From Mental Power to Muscle Power – Gaining Strength by*

Using the Mind, 2004). Isn't that incredible? In order to make the most of this ability of our brain, we should combine physical exercise with visualizations. What you can do is, before your client starts a new exercise, you can ask them to visualize it in as much detail as possible. If they feel unsure about their ability to stick to a new routine, ask them to visualize that routine on a regular basis. Remember that your client doesn't need to only visualize the end result or the "victory," but they should also imagine the details related to the process. This way, they can imagine themselves overcoming their challenges, which can help build their "resilience" muscle.

Use Social Persuasion to Your Client's Advantage

When building our client's self-efficacy, we can use "social persuasion" to their advantage. We've already discussed the importance of affirmations (both self-directed and those that come from us) in building their self-efficacy. We can also help them form groups that can motivate them and keep them accountable during their sessions and beyond. One of the major challenges that many people face in the beginning is in keeping the momentum going after a session. They might be very motivated and energetic in your presence, but have difficulty sticking to their plans if you're not around. Having an "accountability buddy" or even a group can help them overcome this challenge.

If your clients are social media-savvy, you can also help them become a part of online communities that can support them on this journey. Of course, social media should always be used judiciously. You should ensure that your client is part of an inclusive and considerate group, otherwise they'll likely feel more demotivated after their sessions. The same goes for "social comparisons." If your client can use another person's success story to believe in themselves, nothing like it. However, if they get caught up in envy or become demotivated thinking that they're not doing enough—this tactic might work against them. Therefore, it's extremely important to assess how your client reacts to group dynamics and social media before using these tools. Another simple thing you can do is have a board (either online or offline) where you share an inspirational story per month, of one person among the group you coach. When your clients can see not only this person's success, but also their challenges and setbacks—they might believe that they can overcome their own limitations as well. This way, they won't feel targeted either, and might even engage in a little healthy competition to end up on the board next month.

When managed well, social support can become one of the most powerful ways for your client to build self-efficacy. In fact, research has found that social support might even help reduce the impact of our genetic and environmental susceptibility to physical and mental illness, and make us more resilient during times of stress (Ozbay et al., 2007).

Tackling Some Other Barriers to Physical Activity

Often, when we want to achieve a particular goal, we spend a lot of time thinking about the barriers we might encounter along the way. While it's important to be aware of these barriers, it's equally important to not use them as excuses on our journey. As a coach, you need to spend a lot of time understanding and validating the challenges your client faces, while also brainstorming solutions that can help them embrace change. Let's discuss a few of the most common barriers that your client might face on their fitness journey:

- **Lack of time:** Many clients worry about finding the time to exercise if they're already too busy. Encourage them to think of ways of using their existing schedule to make time for exercise. For instance, they don't need to think in terms of huge chunks of time—like an hour—but they can look for 4 slots of 15 minutes throughout the day. Similarly, if thinking about "exercising" seems too intimidating, encourage them to think in terms of "movement." How can they incorporate more movement into their existing schedule? Can they walk to certain places instead of using transport, for instance? Additionally, help them reframe "distractions" as tools to help them reach their goals. For example, if they have to spend time with their kids, why not involve them in fun activities that will also help your client achieve their goals?

- **Health concerns or physical limitations:** If your client tells you that they have a health concern, it's important to not dismiss those concerns. In fact, you should encourage them to be transparent with both you and their health provider at all times. Work with your client to come up with a routine that helps them manage their conditions better. There's an interesting study that tells us how physical activity can help prevent and even delay the onset of many chronic diseases (Booth et al., 2012). Therefore, helping your clients to stay active in whatever way they can, may be key to keeping some of their symptoms in check.

- **Dissatisfaction with results:** Many clients believe that exercising does not give them the results they seek from it, while others give up before they see any real change in themselves. This is why you need to keep revisiting your goals with your clients, and ensure that their goals and milestones are not influenced by other people's journeys or stories in the media. At the same time, you should help them focus on the positive aspects of their journey. For example, they might not have reached their ideal weight yet, but have they started feeling more energetic or sleeping better? If yes, then they have more than enough reasons to celebrate. Last but not least, help your client look at fitness as a way of life. In the beginning, it's understandable that they focus on their immediate goals—as it helps build motivation for the next stretch of their journey. Over time, however, they should be able to see both the highs and lows as part of a lifelong commitment to health.

In this chapter, we've learned how motivational interviewing can help people overcome their barriers to regular exercise. At the same time, we know that good exercise is only one part of the deal. In the next chapter, we'll be using the same tools to make healthy eating less of a punishment and more of an empowering (and fun!) choice for our clients.

A Quick Note from Alec Rowe

Hey there,

If you're finding value in this book, I'd really appreciate a quick favor. Your review can help others discover these strategies and support my work as an independent author.

Just a few words from you on the platform you purchased this book from would mean a lot – it's a huge boost for a book like this and helps build our community.

And if you don't have time for a review at the moment, for now, please just leave a star rating if you've found these pages helpful.

Thanks for your support and for being part of this journey!

Best, Alec

Chapter 5
Motivational Interviewing in Nutrition and Weight Loss

Let's start this chapter with a sobering statistic: A whopping 69% of adults in the U.S. are either overweight or obese (Flegal et al., 2012). That's a little more than two-thirds of the entire adult population. Over the past decade or so, the situation has likely worsened. There are many reasons behind this disturbing trend—including rising stress levels and increasingly sedentary lifestyles—but the most important one is poor diet. In fact, the western diet—also known as the Standard American Diet—is often rich in ultraprocessed foods and poor in whole foods. This leads to a whole host of health issues—both mental and physical—in a majority of the population.

Another concerning aspect of this trend is that there are many forces conspiring against us on our path to good health. For one, many food companies want us to stay dependent on highly processed foods—which is why they use all sorts of chemical additives to make those foods seem irresistible to us. The next time you wonder why you always crave your favorite cookies or chips, remember that food companies have tried very hard to engineer these cravings within all of us. Add to that the onslaught of marketing around these foods, and the common idea that these foods are the only solution for those who are either too busy or on a budget—and we have an entire nation with worrying food habits (more on these trends soon).

As coaches, it's our responsibility to understand the challenges that our clients face each day on their path to healthy eating. In this chapter, we'll learn to use motivational interviewing techniques to help our clients make healthy and nutritious choices for themselves.

Addressing Common Barriers to Healthy Eating

Let's begin by understanding the most common barriers that many people face while trying to eat healthy on a regular basis. We can do this by paying close attention to any use of "sustain talk" by our clients.

Example 1: Healthy foods are boring or lacking in taste.

This could mean one of two things. Either your client has been scared into thinking this way by people around them—or by the portrayal of "healthy foods" in media—or they've actually tried to eat something healthy and didn't like the taste.

Example 2: Healthy foods are not easy on the pocket.

Your client might think this way because they feel that "organic" foods are necessarily expensive, or they might have noticed a difference between ordering their favorite junk food and cooking a healthy meal from scratch.

Example 3: Healthy foods take a lot of time to prepare.

Your client might truly believe that having home-cooked meals is healthier for them, but might also feel intimidated at the thought of giving hours of their time to cooking these meals every day.

Example 4: It's very difficult to find the support I need to make changes to my diet.

Your client might come from a culture which has very different eating patterns than the one they're trying to adopt. Or, they might find it uncomfortable to implement their changes because their families or friends might not be as supportive as they would like.

Example 5: I've never had any success with diets, why should this time be any different?

Many clients try various diets without seeing lasting change in their eating behaviors, which decreases their self-efficacy over time. Instead of questioning whether these "diets" are meant for them, they assume that they simply don't have the willpower to achieve their goals.

Before we discuss the solutions to these concerns, let's go through the motivational interviewing techniques that can help us gain the trust of our client. When clients struggle with their eating habits, they're often subjected to shame and ridicule from others. Not only that, but they might blame themselves for lacking the "discipline" needed to become healthy eaters. As their coach, it's extremely vital to not trigger them or exacerbate their feelings of guilt. This is where empathy, open-ended questions, and reflective listening can come to our aid.

Assessing Your Client's Motivation for Change

Here are some types of open-ended questions we can ask our clients to understand their reasons for and against change:

- **Questions regarding their current lifestyle:** These questions need to be asked delicately and without judgment. Keep the focus on how your client feels about their current state, and not on what you think their problems are. For instance, a good question to ask would be "How does your current lifestyle affect you?" Similarly, you can ask them "Is there something about your current lifestyle that you would like to change, and why?"

- **Questions regarding their readiness for change:** Questions like "How ready do you feel to change your lifestyle?" or "What do you think is different about your commitment to change this time around?" You can even gently ask them about the steps they're willing to take to make the changes they want to see in their life. You can also ask your client what they're comfortable with and what they aren't. For instance, you can ask them "How do you feel about using weight as a measure to track your lifestyle?"

- **Questions regarding the challenges they face on their nutritious eating journey:** Again, make sure that you're not causing discomfort to your client. Instead of asking them why they cannot stick to a healthy eating pattern, for instance, you can ask them, "How do you typically make your food choices?" or "What are the factors that influence your eating patterns?"

- **Questions regarding their past successes and hopes for the future:** Remember that we're trying to build our client's self-efficacy at every step of the way. You can do this by asking your client to focus on their past successes. For instance, they might not have been able to stick to the healthy changes they made in the past, but how did they feel when they could implement those changes—even in the short-term? Or, you can ask them, "What is something you thought you couldn't do, but were able to achieve when you last attempted to change your lifestyle?" Similarly, you can help your client lean into hope by asking them something like, "What is a positive change that will happen in your life if you're able to make these changes?" or "How will your life become different if you can achieve your nutrition goals this year?"

- **Questions regarding their values, beliefs, and dreams:** You want to understand who your client is as a person, and why this change is so meaningful to them. For this, you need to help your client dig deep within themselves and think about their core values, beliefs, and aspirations. For instance, you can ask them, "What is most important to you as a person, and how does your health factor in it?" Or, you can ask them, "Can you tell me what an ideal day or week in your life looks like?"

- **Questions regarding your ability to help them:** Your client should be able to tell you what has worked and what hasn't in the past, and they should also give you ideas about how you can help them in the present. For instance, you can ask them, "What do you need from me to help you succeed?" Or, you can ask them, "What does an ideal coaching session look like to you?" These questions don't mean that you're unsure about your abilities. Instead, they help your client advocate for their own needs during these sessions.

Creating the Decisional Balance Sheet

Since our clients are usually in a state of ambivalence regarding their eating patterns, we can help them create their "decisional balance sheet" to be able to weigh the pros and cons of the decisions they might make, or even to understand the consequences of maintaining status quo. Usually, your client might have trouble weighing the long-term benefits of healthy eating with the short-term sacrifices they'll have to make. For instance, they likely already know that incorporating more fruits and vegetables in their diet will help them in various ways. At the moment, though, it can be extremely overwhelming for them to think about replacing the diet they already have. The meals they currently have might be quicker to prepare, less expensive (at least on the surface), and delicious enough to handle their cravings.

Similarly, a client might really want to eat healthy and shop more consciously, but they don't know where to look for relevant information without feeling intimidated. Encourage them to openly discuss whatever barriers they might be facing on their journey. Then, you can create a list where your client notes down the short-term and long-term costs of their decisions, as well as the immediate and lasting benefits they might receive.

Let's take an example. If your client wants to eat less ultraprocessed foods, the short-term benefits could be an increase in energy and satiety. This is because most of these foods are dense in calories but not in nutrients. Therefore, they can cause an energy spike followed by a crash—which can leave them irritable and fatigued. Having whole foods that are packed with nutrients can counter that. In the long run, a diet rich in whole foods might lead to strength, vitality, and longevity, and even reduce your client's visits to the hospital. In the short term, however, ultraprocessed foods might offer them an easy and hassle-free solution for their cravings. They might have difficulty finding alternatives for the same. They might also worry about having to change their schedule and put in effort toward healthy eating.

This short-term cost could be weighing most heavily on them, and taking away the focus from all the benefits that the change might bring. When you discuss the long-term costs with them, however, your client might realize that there aren't any. For example, they might realize that their healthcare costs will go down if they stick to a whole foods diet.

They might also understand that they can master their cravings after some time, and genuinely start to enjoy "healthy" foods. Not only that, but their health can help them spend more time with those they love, and enjoy their favorite activities for much longer. In other words, the short-term costs can become much less problematic once your client understands that the overall benefits are immense. Visualization exercises are great when creating this decisional balance sheet.

Reflective Listening and Problem-Solving

We've talked about some of the common barriers your client might face on their "healthy eating" journey. In this section, we'll discuss ways to validate your client's concerns and also help them look for possible alternatives in their current situation.

The first thing to do is to validate how your client is feeling when they tell you about their challenges. For example, if they're saying they do not have time to devote to healthy eating, you cannot dismiss it by saying something like, "You'll make time for it if you really want to." Not only will that be unhelpful, but it will also make them defensive around you. Instead, you can say something like, "I can see that you really want to make time for healthy meals, but it's difficult to balance these efforts with your other, equally important responsibilities." Once you've gained their trust, they'll be more welcoming of any suggestions you make to solve their problems.

Since healthy eating can be such a huge change for your clients, help them focus on the "one thing" they can do almost immediately. For instance, if they're worried that they have no time to prepare healthy meals, ask them how long they think it would take for them to prepare a meal. There's a huge chance that they're overestimating the time it might take for them to cook a meal, and if you work with them to find quick recipes, they'll be excited about trying them out. Similarly, if your client doesn't want to keep track of all the nutritional information they can find on food labels, ask them to choose one thing they would like to work on. For example, if they want to reduce their consumption of sugar, that's all they have to look for on food labels.

There's one thing that can help your client overcome multiple problems—lack of time, worrying about costs, and keep healthy foods interesting—meal planning and prep. While meal planning and prep can seem like a huge commitment in the beginning, it actually saves a lot of time, money, and energy down the line. We've talked about how food companies work hard to make unhealthy foods irresistible to us. This is also evident in our grocery stores. If we pay attention, we'll find that ultraprocessed foods are usually stocked at eye level, in central aisles, and near the checkout counters. This is because they work best as impulse buys, which means they need to be always in our line of vision and on our mind. This is also why you might never list these items when making your grocery list but always end up buying them in the store.

Therefore, as important as it is to create a grocery list beforehand, it's equally vital to know how to consciously navigate the grocery store. Also, when you and your client plan for the meals they'll be making in the week ahead, they can use it as an opportunity to get creative. For instance, they can try to use the same base ingredients for multiple meals, which will save them time on meal prep. Similarly, they can learn how to use leftovers from one meal to create their next meal. As they get more creative with meal prep, they'll be surprised by the variety of meals they can conjure with a limited set of ingredients. Preparing for meals beforehand can also help reduce wastage—and hence, save money—because we can then buy only what we truly need. Apart from this, encouraging your client to buy in bulk when needed, and buying frozen foods when possible, can also help them save on both time and money when preparing meals.

Another major barrier that people face in adopting healthy eating habits is the lack of taste. There are two problems related to this. For one, when we're used to eating ultraprocessed foods, we find it difficult to appreciate whole foods. At the same time, we might have a narrow understanding of what healthy food constitutes. Therefore, you can work with your client to expand their definition of healthy food. Healthy food doesn't have to be bland, and the best way to ensure this is by familiarizing ourselves with herbs and spices. Not only do they add flavor to any meal, but they're also healthy alternatives to most of the sugar-laden sauces and condiments we find in stores. Most importantly, let your client give themselves the time needed to wean themselves off ultraprocessed foods. After a while, they'll be able to appreciate the natural flavors of whole foods.

Helping Your Client Be Receptive to Change

Since our eating patterns are so deeply ingrained in us, it can feel like we're making huge sacrifices when trying to overcome these patterns. As long as we think like this, we'll be hesitant to make these changes or eager to revert to our previous patterns. So much so, that some people might think that they're losing out on something important by embracing these healthy behaviors. When food is so intricately linked to our identity, our role as a coach is to not threaten this identity even while trying to create a new one. How do we do this? By encouraging our clients to use their established habits to create new ones.

For example, if your client doesn't want to go from having their favorite cereal for breakfast to having fruits, why not suggest that they add pieces of fruit to cereal? Similarly, if your client likes a sweet treat every now and then, encourage them to try different ingredients—such as pure honey, maple syrup, and jaggery—that are both sweet and nutritionally dense. When your client begins to see change as "addition" or "stacking" rather than "subtraction" or "deprivation," they'll be much more enthusiastic about it.

A Realistic and Empathetic Approach to Body Image Concerns

A challenge many fitness coaches can face is in understanding their client's true relationship with their body. Since diet and fitness culture has gained popularity, it's usually seen as a healthy choice if someone wants to lose weight or "eat better." It can become really tricky to distinguish between people who have a healthy relationship with their body and want to take better care of themselves, from those who want to "fix" themselves because they cannot accept who they are.

A person's body image depends on a lot of things, including their skin, features, and weight. Our body image can also be shaped by the culture we've grown up in, and the environmental and social pressures we're subjected to. For instance, if someone belongs to a culture where people with less body fat are termed as "skinny" or "famished," they'll likely grow up with body image issues, even though they might be deemed attractive in other cultures.

In general, there are four aspects of body image—cognitive, affective, perceptual, and behavioral. Cognitive body image is all about how you *think* about your body. Do you think that you could have lived a better or easier life if you looked a different way? Affective body image tells you how you *feel* about your body. Do you feel happy in your own skin? Do you like every aspect of yourself, or are you sad or disappointed about certain parts of your body? Perceptual body image is all about how you *see* yourself, and this might be completely different from how you are or how others see you. For instance, you might be completely healthy and fit according to your doctor but still see yourself as unhealthy. Similarly, you might be complimented for your skin but have difficulty believing those compliments. Behavioral body image tells you how you *act* because of your body image. For instance, if you want to undergo a cosmetic procedure because you think something's wrong with your face or body, you might be suffering from behavioral issues related to your body image.

Body image can feel like a fitness issue—and it certainly can be—but it's also a mental health concern. Our body image has a lot to do with our self-worth. When we think that we're not "thin enough" or "attractive enough," we're telling ourselves that we don't deserve love, respect, and compassion unless we change ourselves. We tell ourselves that, if only we became someone other than ourselves, we'll finally be good enough for ourselves and for the world. Needless to say, low self-worth can lead to issues such as anxiety, depression, guilt, and shame. In many cases, it can also lead to body dysmorphia—a condition in which people are overly focused on their perceived flaws. I say "perceived" because these flaws don't have to be real. Instead, they are often a reflection of how we're treated by others, what we see in the media, and what we think of ourselves in general. A study showed that body image—especially perceived body image—can be much more damaging to our emotional and mental health than being overweight. What's more, people who are dissatisfied with their bodies are usually at higher risk of developing behavioral issues (Ren et al., 2018).

What are some alternatives to negative body image? In general, we want to promote "body acceptance" in our clients. Body acceptance can be of three kinds—body positivity, body neutrality, and body liberation. While body positivity is all about embracing ourselves and exuding confidence at all times, body neutrality empowers us in a different way. Some people prefer to detach themselves from their body image as much as possible. Meaning, they don't attach positive or negative qualities to their bodies. Similarly, body liberation is more about celebrating the diversity in bodies and promoting body autonomy. What is common to these states of being is a sense that we should accept and support our bodies as much as possible.

Recognizing Symptoms of Body Dissatisfaction in Your Clients

There are two main things to keep in mind as a fitness coach. You need to ensure that your client has a healthy and loving relationship with their body, even when they're trying to become healthier. Additionally, you need to make sure that you're not unintentionally fueling any body image issues—or related unhealthy behaviors—in your clients. Let's look at some signs that you need to watch out for:

- Does your client have a pattern of weight cycling or frequent dieting?
- Does your client usually speak negatively about their body?
- Does your client spend a lot of time on social media—especially on sites that are image-heavy?
- Does your client focus too much on improving their appearance or looking a certain way, even if it might not be the healthiest thing for them?
- Do they use compassionate language when talking about their "failures" in the past, or are they overly dismissive of themselves?
- Are their motivations for losing weight based on their desire to lead a healthy life, or do they want social validation?
- Are their nutrition and fitness goals realistic? For instance, do they want to lose weight quickly, even if it might be dangerous for them? Or do they want to survive on a juice cleanse for the next few weeks in order to look good for an event?

Helping Your Clients Embrace Themselves

Here are a few ways by which you can encourage your clients to achieve body acceptance in their lives:

- **Practice empathetic listening at all times:** Many people who suffer from body image issues have difficulty finding the support they need to improve their self-worth. Therefore, as a coach, you should make them feel safe, especially when they're talking about their vulnerabilities.

- **Help your client identify their triggers:** Poor body image is usually linked to certain triggers that can lead to a negative spiral. Therefore, encouraging your clients to keep an "emotions journal" can help them recognize their negative self-talk and use affirmations to counter them.

- **Help your client move away from social comparisons:** This can, of course, be easier said than done. However, you can help by setting an example for your client and comparing them with only the previous version of themselves. People who suffer from body dissatisfaction might not benefit from social persuasion. In fact, they might need to focus exclusively on their own journey, at least in the beginning.

- **Ensure that your client's goals are realistic and compassionate:** It's understandable that you want your clients to push themselves a little, but they should not be punishing themselves under the guise of self-improvement. If your client sets goals that are unrealistic and even unhealthy for them, gently nudge them by asking open-ended and non-judgemental questions about their decision. Even the framing of their goals becomes important at this time, as the language they use should be compassionate.

- **Let your client see how their body supports them every day:** If your client thinks that "beauty" or "fitness" are the only real measures of their body's worth, they're setting themselves up for an endless cycle of disappointment and self-rejection. Instead, help them see how their body holds them and nurtures them, even on the days when they don't feel healthy. People with chronic illnesses, for example, might have a tougher time appreciating their bodies, but this is an opportunity for them to recognize their body's resilience.

- **Encourage them to seek medical help, if needed:** In case your client shows extreme symptoms of body dysmorphia, anxiety, or depression—they might benefit from professional help. As a coach, you can help them see the value of therapy and the possibility of asking for help.

Through this chapter, we've understood how motivational interviewing can significantly impact your client's nutrition, weight loss, and management goals. We've also discovered that many of these goals are related to mental and emotional health concerns. In the next chapter, we'll learn about using our MI skills to help clients improve their overall mental well-being.

Chapter 6
Motivational Interviewing in Psychology

The good life is a process, not a state of being. –Carl Rogers

If there's a universal goal that seems unattainable to many, it's the pursuit of happiness. So complex is this process that most of us cannot even reach a consensus on the true definition of happiness. It's also true that some of us have a harder time navigating life than others. As such, we need extra support and encouragement as we try to live a healthier and more balanced life.

One of the major challenges that people face on their mental health journey is judgment from those around them. Sometimes, this behavior extends to mental health professionals as well. Think of it this way. In traditional therapeutic relationships, the doctor or therapist sees themselves as an expert, which often leads to them dismissing their patient's opinions or concerns. When it comes to mental health, there's an added layer of stigma that patients need to deal with. Many therapists and coaches act like people with mental health struggles have "failed at life." Instead of being a compassionate and nurturing relationship, the therapist-patient relationship often leads to added guilt and shame in the patient.

Motivational interviewing can help change this, as it's based on the spirit of evocation, collaboration, and autonomy. We should also remember that MI was initially developed as part of an addiction recovery program for alcoholics. Therefore, it can be highly effective in the treatment of anxiety, depression, eating disorders, and substance use disorders. In this chapter, we'll learn how to use MI techniques to help your clients open up about their mental health struggles and provide with them the support they need to build a better life for themselves.

Benefits of Motivational Interviewing for Mental Health

Here are a few benefits of using MI techniques to help your clients improve their mental health:

- It provides a safe space for clients to talk about their deepest fears and insecurities.
- It helps the therapists treat their clients as partners on this journey, thus building a deeper and more powerful connection with them.
- It helps patients understand why change is necessary in their lives, and also empowers them to create the change they seek in themselves.
- Through MI, patients usually become more receptive to the idea of seeking treatment.
- Since MI helps build a patient's self-efficacy, it helps them gain the confidence needed to stick to their treatment plan.
- MI also helps the patients take accountability for their emotions, behaviors, and challenges.

Using Motivational Interviewing to Help Your Client Navigate Life's Twists and Turns

Even if your client doesn't suffer from mental health issues in general, they might face certain challenges in their life that increase their stress and anxiety levels. In fact, your client doesn't necessarily need to deal with trauma or loss to be stressed or anxious. Certain life transitions—such as getting a new job, moving into a new city, beginning a new relationship, or becoming a parent for the first time—can overwhelm and unsettle them. At this time, they might need a "transition coach" to feel supported. When they don't have the support they need during these times, they begin to see change as something undesirable and even unpleasant. As a transition coach, you can help them see change as a necessary and positive thing in their journey.

Here are a few things you can do to make transitions seem less intimidating to your clients:

- If your client is still weighing the pros and cons of making the transition—in cases where they have a choice in the matter—help them **create a decisional balance sheet** to make an informed decision.

- Ensure your client that **it's perfectly okay to feel nervous** before, and during, a big life change.

- If your client feels extremely worried about the possible negative effects of change, **ask them open-ended questions that help them explore the costs of maintaining status quo**. For instance, while it might be true that your client's new workplace is challenging or underwhelming, it's certainly true that their current workplace has nothing more to offer them. Wouldn't it be better for them to take a chance and see what their new workplace has to offer them?

- **Help your client see stress as a positive force in their lives**. Of course, it's important for them to manage their stress effectively, but they should also be able to see stress as an indicator that they're involved in something meaningful in their lives. For instance, if they're going to become a parent, it's perfectly natural for them to feel stressed, but this stress comes with the promise of joy, love, and growth for the entire family.

- Help your client create a **main plan and a backup plan** for this phase. Since your client's world is in a state of flux at this time, they can expect more than a few surprises. Having a contingency plan will put their mind at ease, and help them focus on the positives of the transition.

- Figure out ways to **help your client manage stress** during this phase. You can conduct mindfulness sessions that help your client stay connected to themselves in the present moment, and you can also help them identify and lean on their support network when needed.

Encouraging Your Clients to Challenge Their Negative Behavioral Patterns

If your client suffers from behavioral issues, they might be hesitant to seek help from you in the beginning. This is because they're used to being judged by others, and hence take a defensive stance throughout the conversation. This is when you need to exercise empathy instead of judgment, and compassion instead of pity. Your client should feel respected at all times, even as they discuss their issues and past mistakes with you.

Exploring Your Client's Resistance

Begin by asking your client certain open-ended questions to understand why they're resisting change. For instance, if your client feels like therapy isn't going to be of much help to them, ask them why they think so. They might tell you something like, "Well, my last few attempts at therapy haven't really shown results," or "I don't think I have it in me to stick to a treatment plan." If your client is still engaging in "sustain talk," you need to ask them why they're considering therapy again.

Evoking Change Talk Within Your Client

Your client will engage in "change talk" when they begin to uncover their own motivations for change. For instance, you could ask them to talk about the highlights of their previous sessions. Even if things went downhill in the end, was there a time when they were doing well? What would make it easier for your client to stick to their treatment plan? Help them focus on the future, on past successes, and on alternative options for the present.

Engaging With Your Client Using Affirmations, Reflections, and Summaries

When your client begins to open up to you, make sure that they know you're firmly on their side. For instance, if they tell you that they were doing well in therapy until there was an incident at home that triggered them, let them sit in that realization for a while. You can then reflect their thoughts and feelings back to them by saying something like, "It can be difficult to commit to therapy when you're feeling angry or upset by things that are happening at home. However, kudos to you for getting so far and for trying again." This way, you not only affirm their efforts, but also acknowledge the challenges they face in the quest for change.

This might prompt your client to open up a little more about their situation. They could say something like, "When things get unstable at home, my first priority is to protect my younger siblings, but I wish I had someone to lean on during these times." At this point, your client is hinting at their need for a support group. Again, you can affirm their efforts by saying, "It must take a lot of courage and patience to be there for your siblings when you're triggered." At the same time, you can also summarize your conversation by saying, "From what I understand, you really want to stay committed to therapy, but it gets difficult when things are unstable at home and you're the only one protecting your siblings. It might help to have someone in your corner during this time."

This summary can either prompt your client to ask about support groups they can join, or it can set the stage for you to offer advice to them. As you probably know by now, MI practitioners don't believe in directive guidance in general. In fact, directive guidance—in which the counselor or coach offers advice or information—is usually the basis of traditional therapeutic relationships. At the same time, there might be some points in your MI-based relationship where your client might expect you to provide them information or advice. How do we do this in a way that keeps the spirit of MI intact?

Providing Information or Advice to Your Client

Since Miller and Rollnick wanted MI-based therapy to move away from the traditional mentor-mentee or expert-novice relationships, they came up with the "elicit-provide-elicit" framework for practitioners to use. The most important part of this framework is to always seek permission from the client before giving them any advice or information. Don't assume that you know what the client needs.

Step 1: Elicit: At this stage, you need to ask your client if they need any advice or information that you think might help them.

Step 2: Provide: Give them the information they need in simple language. Don't overcomplicate things, and make sure that your knowledge isn't coming in the way of their comprehension.

Step 3: Elicit: Ask your client if they understood what you told them, or if they need further clarification. Depending on their answer, you either stop at this stage or provide them with the necessary information.

Let's take an example to understand this approach further. In the previous example, your client has hinted that they might do better if they had a support system to rely on when they're triggered. Here's how you can use this framework in this situation.

Step 1: Elicit: "It seems like you might benefit from having a support system of some kind. Would you like me to suggest some groups that you can be a part of?

Step 2: Provide: If your client says yes, you can give them a few options to choose from. It's also a good idea to ask them whether they would prefer offline or online groups—and to get a sense of their schedule—so that you can offer them the options most suited to them.

Step 3: Elicit: "Do these options work for you? Is there anything else you would like me to help you with?"

Use of Motivational Interviewing in the Treatment of Substance Abuse Disorders

One of the most prevalent mental health disorders around the world is related to substance abuse. Traditionally, therapy for these disorders includes a combination of medication, counseling, and support groups. However, since addiction is a complex issue that is related to personal, social, and familial conditions—there can be a lot of resistance on the part of the patient to make or stick to changes. It also doesn't help that most of traditional therapy can be confrontational and directive in nature. When the therapist has already formed an (often negative) perception of the patient, they advise or reproach the patient instead of trying to understand them. As an MI coach, you can change this dynamic through the **Desire, Ability, Reason, and Need (DARN) model** (*Motivational Interviewing (MI)*, 2024):

- **Explore your patient's desire for change:** Try to understand how deeply the patient desires change, and how much faith they have in the process, through open-ended questions. For instance, you can ask them "What does an ideal day look like for you, and how does your drinking habit feature in it?" Or, "What are some of your expectations from our sessions together?"

- **Figure out how capable your patient is in changing their behaviors:** Ask them about any ideas they might have regarding this process. What are some methods that have helped them in the past, and how confident are they about overcoming their problems?

- **Talk them through their motivations for change and the reasons that are holding them back:** At this stage, you need to understand what specifically motivates or deters your patient on this journey. Questions such as, "What are some of the reasons you've decided to stop drinking?" or "What has kept you from achieving your goals in your last few attempts?"

- **Understand how urgent their need for change is:** We want to know how ready and willing our patients are to commit to the process of change. An addiction recovery program is usually very demanding, and there are high chances of relapse. Therefore, it's important to help the patient visualize what they're trying to achieve through the process. For instance, you can ask them something like, "What do you stand to lose if things continue the way they are?" or "Why is it important for you to make the change right now?"

The DARN model should help your patient get ready for change. Once they show enough motivation to change—and you're both aligned on the goals of the program—you can help them plan for change using the **Commitment, Activation, and Taking Steps (CAT) model** (*Motivational Interviewing (MI)*, 2024):

WORDS THAT WORK

- **Commitment:** In this stage, you want your patient to show commitment toward specific actions. There should be minimal ambivalence at this stage. How can you ensure that your client is committed to change? Ask them questions about their next steps. Look out for statements like, "I am going to make these changes in my life" or "I intend to implement these steps in my daily routine." We're moving away from "should," "can," or "want" statements.

- **Activation:** This stage tells us that our patient is ready and willing to take the actual steps needed to overcome their substance use behaviors. Here, your client's statements could sound like, "I'm ready to start working on this plan from tomorrow." Here, the goals become more immediate and your client starts making concrete and well-defined plans.

- **Taking steps:** At this stage, your client has started taking the steps necessary for change, and they might even have some preliminary feedback for you. For instance, they could talk about all the steps they've taken in the current week to achieve their goals, or they could talk about the emotions they experience when they implement these steps.

Here are a few things to keep in mind when dealing with patients struggling with substance abuse disorders:

- It's extremely important for you to **build a rapport** with your patient. This is true for any behavioral change process, but in the case of substance abuse, your patient really needs to trust you and be vulnerable with you. Understand that if they don't feel safe with you, these sessions could become a different kind of trigger for them.

- At all times, you need to monitor the **side effects** associated with substance use, as well as the potential **withdrawal symptoms** that set in once your patient starts their road to recovery. Both of these can complicate their recovery process and make it that much harder for them to follow through on their commitments.

- Pay attention to your **patient's triggers**. When your patient is trying to change their behaviors, they'll have to learn how to manage their triggers in real time, or they can undo weeks of hard work in an instant. Only when we know our patient's triggers can we help them identify coping mechanisms that work for them.

- Give equal importance to their **personal goals and cultural context**. While it's extremely important that your client knows why they want to change, it's also vital to examine their goals, behaviors, and challenges against their cultural and familial background. This doesn't mean that we let our biases creep in. In fact, we need to work hard to question and overcome any inherent biases we might have regarding a person's substance abuse history.

- Be open to discussing **lots of alternatives** for their treatment. Addiction recovery can be complex, and needs to be tailored to each individual. What works for one person might not work at all for someone else. Instead of seeing this as a failure on your or your patient's part, look at it as a way to find unique solutions for your patient. Not only does this help them, but it also expands your own understanding of substance abuse—thus making you a more empathetic therapist.

- Explore options for providing **social support** to your patient wherever possible. Since social factors can affect your patient's triggers as well as their response to recovery, it's important to help them build a social network that makes them feel safe and understood. You might need to help them identify the people they can lean on and those who might interfere with or complicate their recovery. Of course, this needs to be done with as much empathy and compassion as possible.

While this is true for any change process, it helps immensely to remember it in case of addiction recovery: We always target the problem, and not the client or patient.

The FRAMES Approach in Motivational Interviewing

While we're discussing this approach here, it can be used in the fields of physical fitness, nutrition, and mental health improvement with equal ease. For practitioners who are starting out, this approach can help them determine the steps they need to take to ensure they're being supportive of their clients (Kamya, 2012).

- **F: Feedback**—When your client is still debating whether to change or not, you might need to provide them feedback regarding the consequences of choosing the status quo. This becomes even more important when your client stands to suffer from health issues by not embracing change. For example, if they are a heavy smoker, they need to quit so that their lungs and heart are protected. Even though they know this, it's your role as a coach to elicit this "change talk" within them by giving them timely and respectful feedback. Keep in mind that your feedback should not be subjective in any way. You need to rely on facts, medical reports, and studies to convince your client that choosing to change will benefit them.

- **R: Responsibility**—The responsibility of embracing change always lies with the client, and they should know this at all times. At no point should your client feel forced or disempowered. Once you've given them the facts, you need to step back and let them decide for themselves. That's the only way that the changes they make will stick.

- **A: Advice**—As we've mentioned earlier, we can only offer advice if our client explicitly asks us for it. Again, advice should always keep the client in mind, and it should be up to them to accept or reject it.

- **M: Menu**—One of the best ways of empowering your client is by offering them a menu of choices. Even when you're planning their next steps, you should give them a lot of options to choose from. This helps your client see that there are different ways of approaching the same problem, and that they don't have to choose something that doesn't work for them.

- **E: Empathy**—There are many times during your sessions when your client might act irritable or disappointed. They might even project some of their own frustrations on you. It's easy to practice empathy when your client is being forthcoming or friendly, but it can be difficult to understand them when they're being "difficult." The usual approach to empathy is that we should understand how our client feels when they talk to us about their problems. Even if we cannot emotionally resonate with them, we can certainly work on our cognitive empathy skills. I would like to suggest another, slightly radical, way. What if we assumed that we can *never understand* how our client is feeling—no matter how many books we read or how many similar experiences we have? What if we use this understanding to become much better listeners—not taking anything they say for granted, not telling ourselves that we "get them?" What if we listen only to learn?

- **S: Self-efficacy**—No matter how under-confident your client might seem when they come to you for coaching, you have to build their self-efficacy. It can be tempting for you to take on the emotional and mental work they need to do to make things easier for them. While some clients might be grateful that you're "helping" them, they're the ones who lose out in the long run. Therefore, don't let your compassion toward your client prevent you from empowering them—even if it means taking a step back every now and then.

In the last few chapters, we've seen how motivational interviewing techniques can help improve your clients' mental and physical health, as well as their overall sense of well-being. Now, we need to understand how to measure the effectiveness of our MI-based coaching sessions, which we'll be doing in the next chapter.

Chapter 7
Measuring Success and Evaluating Outcomes

When you're starting out as a coach, it can be very overwhelming to think of the impact you can have on your clients. It's perfectly natural to worry about your own efficacy in this role. Before we discuss some of the ways in which you can measure your success as a coach, it's vital to understand what success looks like in coaching and therapy.

Coaching is all about hope and transformation. As a coach, you can help your client realize their personal and professional goals, lead a more fulfilling life, change some of their unhealthy behaviors, and even get closer to self-realization. In some cases, coaches can also encourage clients to create meaningful social change in their communities. What's more satisfying than empowering someone else through coaching, right? While it's important to have some concrete measures of how we're doing in our practice, we should not forget about the many intangible benefits that our coaching can provide others.

Importance of Measuring Your Client's Progress

Measuring the progress made by our client is essentially a way of measuring your own progress as a coach. As well-intentioned as we might be, many of us tend to overestimate the positive impact we have on our clients, and underestimate the mistakes we've made along the way. Also, put yourself in your client's shoes for a bit. No one likes to assume that they're not doing a good job, which is why we can become defensive when thinking about our mistakes and weaknesses. A great way to combat these feelings is by keeping the focus entirely on your client. Since you're invested in their success, you can simply track how they've been doing, and use it as a measure to determine your own progress.

There is a caveat attached to this method, however. While we need to look at our client's progress as an indication of what we're doing right and what we can do better, we should not over-identify with our clients. This is especially true in cases where we feel a kinship with them. There might be times when our clients relapse or struggle, and that's not always a comment on our coaching skills. Of course, it takes a while for us to achieve this level of security. So, if in the beginning, you find yourself overly affected by your client's progress, give yourself the time needed to "feel your feelings," and then move on.

Here are a few questions that can help you determine whether you've made a positive impact on your client's life:

- Has the client learned something new about themselves or the world around them, through your coaching sessions?

- Has the client learned emotional intelligence skills by becoming more aware of their own and others' emotions?

- Have you enriched the client's life in some way? Do these learnings enhance their life in any way?

- Has your client gained a new perspective on life through these coaching sessions?

- Is your client better able to engage with the world around them? Are they able to take in relevant information without getting too overwhelmed?

- Is your client more confident about their ability to make good decisions?

- Does your client have a greater sense of accountability for their life now than they did before?

- Is your client able to report the changes in their own life due to these coaching sessions?

- Can their family members, friends, or other trusted associates vouch for the improvements in their life?

- Can your client determine their strengths and weaknesses, and talk to you about possible areas of improvement?

- Does your client see this experience as a success in at least one aspect?

As you can see, there is more than one way for your client to achieve success on their journey.

Measuring the Benefits of Motivational Interviewing on Clients

You can also create a tracker or journal for yourself, in which you make a note of the various short-term and long-term benefits that you want your clients to enjoy. Here are a few short-term benefits that you can hope to achieve:

- greater focus to achieve their goals,
- improved self-efficacy,
- reduced ambivalence and resistance,
- greater motivation and commitment to change,
- building a strong rapport with you,
- accountability for their behaviors and feelings,
- greater vulnerability and trust,
- higher engagement levels,
- willingness to make a plan and stick to it, and
- more faith in their decision-making abilities.

You can add more benefits to this list according to your personal experiences and the situation at hand. Similarly, there are a few long-term benefits that your client can enjoy if you do a good job as their coach:

- moving away from instant gratification,
- being able to see things from a holistic point of view, and not giving in to extremes,
- gaining perspective in various aspects of life,
- being able to apply the learnings from one area of their lives into another,
- improved sleeping patterns and diet, and a healthier overall lifestyle,
- better mental health,
- ability to be resilient when faced with difficulties,
- better quality of life—whatever that means to them,
- being able to make sustainable changes to their lifestyle,
- becoming less prone to relapses and breaking free of lifelong patterns, and
- discovering a way of life that is true to their core values.

While short-term benefits can be monitored if you're still actively coaching your client, you need to come up with ways to check in with your client in the long term. You and your client can determine a schedule that works for both of you. You could, for example, have a monthly check-in session where your client simply talks to you about their current life and the highs and lows they experience. During these sessions, you can simply ask them open-ended questions and then employ active listening to understand how they're dealing with life. Also, remember that your client does not need to be absolutely on top of things. If they've made significant progress in even one area, it deserves to be celebrated.

Different Measures of Success for a Motivational Interviewing Coach

Remember the discussion we had about Miller and Rollnick being wary of too many certifications for MI trainers? For them, the most important aspect of success in MI coaching was the coach's desire to stay true to the spirit of MI. As MI gains more popularity across fields, you'll likely come across a variety of tools to measure your progress. At the same time, it's important to determine which measures matter to you and which don't. Let's take an example here. You might be part of a group where everyone earns very well and holds important positions in prestigious organizations. They're obviously very happy with themselves because they're making progress according to the measures that are valuable to them.

However, you are deeply dissatisfied with your job, even though you're earning well and progressing in your career. This could be because you don't have the same measures of success and happiness as the others in your group. Maybe, you would be happy earning half of what you earn right now, as long as you were doing meaningful work. Even the concept of "meaningful" work might change from person-to-person. You might derive meaning from a role that offers you good work-life balance, while someone else might find it meaningful to spend all their waking hours on a passion project. The point I'm trying to make is, beyond the standardized tests and frameworks lies your own interpretation of success. Keep this in mind as we discuss the different measures that we can use to gauge the impact of our coaching practice.

Motivational Interviewing Results

This measure deals with the outcomes of our motivational interviewing sessions. In order to measure the results of our efforts, we need to measure our client's well-being, satisfaction, engagement, and changes in behavior. We can measure these outcomes by asking them to answer questionnaires or fill in surveys. For example, if we want to understand how much autonomy our client has been provided with during the sessions, we can use the Treatment Self-Regulation Questionnaire. If we want to determine whether our clients are now ready to embrace change, we can use the "readiness ruler."

There are two sides to the readiness ruler—the importance of change to the client, and their confidence about making the change. Both these aspects are measured on a "ruler" that goes from 0 to 10—with "zero" showing that the client is not confident about change or doesn't consider change important, and "ten" showing that they consider change to be very important for themselves, and are very confident about implementing that change in their lives. Of course, a client can consider change highly important and still not be confident enough about their ability to change. When we know this, we can work with our client to increase their self-efficacy over time. Once your client has indicated where they are on the readiness ruler, they need to be asked more open-ended questions that help you understand what their concerns are. For instance, why is it that they consider change to be very important in their lives, but are only somewhat confident about being able to achieve it?

Another measure that helps clients express their satisfaction with the coaching sessions is known as the Client Evaluation of Motivational Interviewing (CEMI). This is a measure that is used to understand whether the client thought their coach exhibited MI consistent behavior. There are 16 aspects that are considered in this measure, such as, "Did the coach help you feel hopeful about changing your behavior?" The client then usually indicates their answer on a 4-point scale that goes from "Not at all" to "A great deal." Of course, this measure also looks at negative items, for instance, "Did the counseling spend time focusing on your weaknesses?" These items are scored in reverse. The higher the CEMI score of the coach, the more MI consistent their behavior is (Madson et al. 2015).

When it comes to feedback, it includes measures like CEMI, but it can also include things like self-reflection, peer review, video and audio recording of sessions, and so on. Basically, you can work with anything that gives you a clear idea of your impact on your client during and after the sessions. After a while, you might also have a community of MI-based coaches who can observe you during some of the sessions, and let you know if there's anything you can improve.

Motivational Interviewing Techniques

Since there are many MI techniques that can be used to help our clients move through the "stages of change," it can be useful to measure the effects of these techniques on your clients. For instance, you might like to assess if you're using "client-centered language" in your interactions with them. Do you properly recognize the difference between "change talk," "sustain talk," "commitment language," or "activation language?" How do you know if your verbal exchanges with your client are helping them resolve their ambivalence and increase their motivation to change? There are certain measures you can use to both identify and assess the language being used in your conversations, such as the Client Language Easy Rating (CLEAR) system, or the Motivational Interviewing Skills Code (MISC) system.

Motivational Interviewing Fidelity and Ethics

For many MI practitioners—including Miller and Rollnick—the coach's intention to stay true to the spirit of MI is more important than almost anything else. While only you can honestly determine whether you're honoring the spirit of MI, there are certain measures that can help you understand how consistently you're adhering to the core MI principles. Similarly, MI ethics tell us that we need to show respect and empathy toward our clients at all times, and that we need to support their autonomy, help them build self-efficacy, and always deal with them in a fair, transparent, and well-intentioned manner. There are many measures that help us keep track of this—including the Motivational Interviewing Treatment Integrity (MITI) code, the International Coaching Federation (ICF) code of ethics, the MINT code of ethics, or the American Psychological Association (APA) code of ethics.

As you progress on your own journey as a coach, you'll likely develop a strong intuitive sense of what works and what doesn't work for both you and your clients. You'll become more confident about choosing clients who sync with you, and those who can benefit most from your coaching style. At the same time, these official measures can help you find your way if you find yourself a little lost or overwhelmed every now and then.

Now that we've discussed how to measure the effectiveness of our coaching practice, let's talk about using everything we've learned so far to build a successful one.

Chapter 8
Building a Successful Coaching Practice

Okay, so you've practiced various motivational interviewing techniques, gotten intimate with the spirit of MI, and even worked with a few clients to better understand your strengths and weaknesses as an MI coach. You're amazed at the wide-ranging applications of MI, and you're wondering about making it a part of your regular coaching practice. Whether you're in the process of establishing a coaching practice for the first time, or if you want to integrate MI techniques into your well-established practice, you need to keep certain things in mind. Let's discuss them in this chapter.

Ensuring a Smooth Transition Into Motivational Interviewing Practices

If your clients are used to a certain therapeutic style—and it works for them—they might understandably be hesitant about your shift to MI-based coaching. Additionally, they might not be aware of how MI works, and why it's superior to traditional coaching in many ways. Since coaching works on trust, you need to ensure that your clients don't feel betrayed due to this transition. It's also vital to understand that many clients are used to the "expert-novice" or "mentor-mentee" relationship that is promoted in traditional therapy. Therefore, when they're told that they can now make decisions for themselves—or that they can lead the coaching sessions—they might have trouble understanding this. They might even feel ill-equipped to handle their newfound autonomy. Therefore, it's best to ease them into the process, and keep a few things in mind:

- **Take some time to help them explore the benefits of MI for themselves:** You can start by asking them about some of the concerns they have regarding your current coaching practice. You can also help them visualize their ideal coaching sessions. More often than not, they will express a need to be empathized with, respected, and empowered. You can then let them know that motivational interviewing treats these things as integral to the coaching practice. Not only that, but you can also talk them through the studies that have shown the effectiveness of MI techniques across various fields.

- **Explain to them that your relationship is evolving for the better:** Your client might worry about being alienated from you because of this transition. If they're used to being told what to do—and that is no longer the case—they might feel abandoned by you. They might also feel like you're no longer invested in their change journey. Therefore, you should help them understand that an MI-based relationship is a lot more intimate than a traditional one. In fact, this relationship treats them as your partner, which can help them become more vulnerable with you. They might need a few sessions to understand how this works, but it's your job to keep the focus firmly on your relationship with them.

- **Keep your approach client-centered at all times:** When you move to an MI-based coaching practice, your client will likely notice a change in the way you talk to them. What should remain the same is your commitment to help the client achieve the life they truly want. For this, you need to focus on their evolving needs, challenges, and goals. Show your client how your aims remain the same—even though your approach has changed—so that they get the confidence needed to work with you in this new environment.

- **Take things slow and steady:** For many clients, this can be a major transition in how they interact with you. Therefore, the more gradual this transition is, the easier it will be for them to embrace it. Look for aspects of MI coaching that are already present in your current coaching practice, and make small changes in areas that are different from your current methods.

- **Check in with your client and ask for regular feedback:** As excited as you might be to implement these changes in your coaching practice—and as much as you'd like to believe that your clients will benefit from it—you need to take their concerns into account. Schedule regular check-in sessions with your clients, ask them what they like about the new processes and what they're still getting used to. Help them see how these new processes can benefit them in the long run, even if they take a while to get used to in the present.

- **Make tough choices if you have to:** Now, this is obviously something you don't want to act on unless absolutely necessary. Ideally, you would like all your clients to transition smoothly into your new practice, but it is possible that some of them are simply not ready for the new techniques. As I mentioned earlier, this could be because they've not been exposed to a client-centric approach till now, or because they have extremely low self-efficacy. You need to ensure that you've tried everything to give them the confidence needed to continue with you. Nevertheless, if they feel like they cannot adjust to your new coaching practice, you might have to let them go. You can also refer them to colleagues you think can work well with them.

As you grow into your coaching career, you want to be known as someone who believes in themselves and their offerings. This doesn't mean that you have to restrict yourself to one niche (though you can do that if you want), but it does mean that you start working on your brand. When people think about the different coaches they can go to, they should be able to identify what it is you offer, and why you're a good bet for them. This can only happen when you are clear about what you can and cannot support.

Identifying the Common Roadblocks You Might Face on Your Coaching Journey

If you've been a coach for some time, and have only just gotten introduced to MI-based practices, you're likely to "relapse" into your old ways every now and then. After all, you're embarking on a "change journey" of your own, so you will encounter roadblocks along the way. This doesn't mean that you're "failing" as an MI coach. All it means is that you need to be aware of the pitfalls so that you can improve yourself over time. This is especially important because—without self-awareness—we might end up sending mixed signals to our clients, which can make it difficult for them to trust us.

Look out for these behaviors when you engage with your clients:

- **Arguing with your client:** When we believe that we need to persuade our client to see our point of view, we often end up smothering them with logic and arguing with them. While we want the best for them, it might come across as if we want to be right more than anything else. In some cases, of course, we might need to provide extra information to our clients, but only if we have taken their permission first. In all other aspects, we trust them to have enough knowledge and intelligence to figure things out for themselves.

- **Using fear-based or authoritative language:** We already know that we shouldn't "direct" our clients at any point of time. We don't need to assume a superior position for them to respect us and do what's best for them. At the same time, make sure that you don't talk about "consequences" when discussing their challenges. This can work in two ways. One, we warn our clients that they can face consequences for not making the change. Two, we warn them about having to face our displeasure or disappointment. The second kind of warning can be given even through nonverbal cues, which is why it's important to monitor both our words and our body language.

- **Disrespecting your client in any way:** This includes blaming, judging, criticizing, or ridiculing your clients—especially as a form of "negative motivation." You don't have to agree with your client at all points (in fact, you shouldn't), but you need to communicate your differences respectfully.

- **Agreeing with your client all the time:** This can sound counterintuitive, especially because we're taught to empathize with our clients as much as possible. At the same time, empathy does not mean agreement or approval. When we agree with our clients all the time, or we show them our approval by praising them constantly—we interrupt the flow of information coming our way. The same goes for reassuring behaviors during a conversation. We want to affirm our client's experience, but we don't want to trivialize their ambivalence by sympathizing with them throughout the conversation. Not only that, but we might need our clients to explore the dissonance they experience between their aspirations and their current behaviors. This can only happen if we let them sit in the uncomfortable feelings that come up every once in a while.

- **Being eager to analyze your client:** Those that have been in this field for a while have likely seen a lot of clients with similar concerns, which can lead to a tendency to "slot" people into categories. Others among us might begin to see people as puzzles to be solved—making us eager to figure them out. While we want to understand their triggers and behavioral patterns, we want them to lead the way. When we force meaning into everything our client tells us, we keep them from becoming truly vulnerable with us.

- **Interrupting your client through well-intentioned methods:** When your client is speaking, you might feel like you've suddenly received an insight that you have to share with them. Or, you might be worried that your client is having difficulty tapping into their emotions—and try to solve the problem by distracting them with a joke or quip. Again, this does not help the client, and might even keep them from connecting with you fully. Don't get me wrong. You can certainly crack jokes with your client and make them feel comfortable before and after the session, but there are times when you simply need to sit with them as they navigate their emotions. This is why reflective listening is so important in MI-based coaching.

- **Preaching to and teaching your client:** In your coaching practice, you'll come across people who have different values and beliefs from you. Many of them might have a way of living that doesn't really resonate with you. If you're trying to work with a client who suffers from anxiety, depression, substance abuse, or eating disorders—they're likely already hard on themselves. It's also possible that their cultural and familial context might be difficult to understand. Still, none of this should be a reason for you to engage in moralizing when dealing with your client. It might even happen unconsciously, so you need to be extra cautious in the beginning. Always remember this mantra: You want to help your client live *their* best life, not yours.

The Importance of Continuous and Lifelong Learning in Motivational Interviewing

While both continuous and lifelong learning are rooted in similar principles, there's a small difference between them that can be beneficial for us to understand. Continuous learning is all about regularly updating our knowledge and skills in a particular field, keeping us relevant and in-demand. It helps us negotiate for higher fees and better working conditions, and also keeps us relatively safe from the uncertainties that can plague our industry. Lifelong learning, though similar, is more about all-round development. In other words, it's about being curious and open in life, and about trying to understand ourselves better through the various experiences we have. A lifelong learner can take almost any situation in their life and use it as an opportunity to grow.

For us to be successful as MI coaches, we need to be both continuous and lifelong learners. There are many ways to achieve continuous learning as an MI coach:

- **Learning at your own pace and in your own style:** If you're someone who takes initiative and is a self-starter, you might be able to learn a lot on your own. You can learn from the plethora of research papers available online, or through podcasts, online tutorials, and books. Not only that, but once you gain confidence in your coaching abilities, you can even experiment a bit with your style. Figure out what works for you and your client, and you might even end up discovering a few strengths you weren't formerly aware of.

- **Learning through formal sources:** You can join a course in a university, become part of a training program, or even find workshops near you. If you have access to someone who has been a successful MI coach for a while, you can also ask them to mentor you if they have time.

- **Social learning:** You can find a community of MI coaches who can offer peer reviews and feedback at regular intervals. You can also use social media to connect with those who are working in different cultural contexts, in order to gain a deeper appreciation for the scope of MI. Once you've gained a fair bit of reputation as an MI coach, why not try and offer mentoring services for those just starting out on their journey?

In order to become a lifelong learner, you simply need to cultivate a growth mindset, and you need to embrace every aspect of this journey with gratitude and hope. After all, you're in the business of making possibilities real, and that's something to be really proud of.

Let's now move on to the conclusion, which helps summarize everything we've learned in this book.

Conclusion

My motivation for this book came from a sobering realization: Even though I was passionate about creating lasting change in my clients' lives, I was unable to keep myself going in the face of numerous challenges. How ironic would it be if a coach lost their motivation for coaching? And yet, this is exactly what was happening. Many of us who want to be coaches know how demanding this work can be. Nevertheless, we seek solace in the fact that our clients' successes are our true rewards. What happens then, when we're unable to give our clients the support and encouragement they need to make changes in their life? Clearly, there is a need for a kind of coaching practice that not only empowers the client but also the coach. This book is a result of extensive research as well as practical experiences that have helped me elevate my coaching practice.

Here are a few things that I hope you've learned through this book:

- In the first chapter, we discussed all about the basics of motivational interviewing. We familiarized ourselves with the spirit and principles of MI, and also discussed the benefits of MI-based coaching.

- In the second chapter, we understood the role of a coach, and the differences between traditional and MI-based coaching. We also talked about the importance of forming a collaborative relationship with our client—through empathy, active listening, and respect.

- In the third chapter, we understood the different motivational interviewing techniques. We focused especially on the development of self-efficacy in our clients. After learning about these core techniques, we discussed using them to help our clients overcome their ambivalence and become motivated to change. We also understood the stages-of-change model, and learned to identify and move away from "sustain talk" in our clients.

- From the fourth chapter onward, we began to apply our learning to various fields of coaching. In the fourth chapter, we focused on using MI-based coaching to help our clients commit to an exercise routine that works for them and makes physical fitness a reality for themselves. We addressed the different barriers that our clients might face on their physical fitness journey, and talked about ways to build their self-efficacy.

- In the fifth chapter, we focused our attention on healthy eating. We recognized the unique challenges that come with making healthy eating a part of our routine, and talked about ways to overcome those challenges. We also learned to help our clients create a "decisional balance sheet" for themselves, so that they can take the steps needed to make change possible. Last but not least, we learned about the body image issues that many of our clients could suffer from, and discussed ways to help them deal with those issues without jeopardizing their quest for change.

- In the sixth chapter, we looked at the applications of MI-based therapy to improve our client's mental and emotional well-being. We talked about the added stress and anxiety that comes with major (and minor) life transitions, and the importance of having a transition coach during these times. Apart from this, we focused on substance abuse disorders and talked about the best ways to help clients who are dealing with these issues. In this chapter, we also explored the DARN-CAT and FRAMES methods to help us on our MI coaching journey.

- After understanding the various applications of MI-based coaching, we learned about measuring the success of our coaching practice in the seventh chapter. We discussed ways to track our client's progress and to measure both the short-term and long-term benefits of motivational interviewing. We also discussed the various measures available to us for tracking our progress as well as fidelity to the spirit of MI.

- The last chapter was all about making MI an integral part of our coaching practice. We discussed ways to make the transition from traditional coaching to MI-based coaching easier on our clients, and we also addressed some of the common roadblocks we might experience on our MI journey. In the end, we learned about the importance of both lifelong and continuous learning in order to be a successful coach.

Now that you have the tools and insights needed to revolutionize your coaching practice through motivational interviewing, what are you waiting for? There's no perfect moment for you to start your journey. Instead, you need to take it one step at a time, and before you know it, you will have transformed not just your clients' lives but also your own. Everything you've ever envisioned for yourself as a coach is now within reach, waiting for you to reach out.

Before you go, my co-author and editor and I have a humble request.

Final Thoughts from Alec Rowe and Jane Kennedy

As we reach the end of our educational journey together, I'd like to ask for a small but impactful favor.

If this book has inspired you to take the next stop in your coaching journey and given you the confidence needed to believe in your abilities, please consider leaving a review. Your feedback not only supports me as an independent author but also guides others to the resources they need for their business journey.

A quick review on the platform you purchased this book can make a significant difference. It helps more people discover and benefit from the content, just like you did.

Thank you for joining me, and for any support you can offer. Your contribution truly matters.

Wishing you continued success,

Alec Rowe and Jane Kennedy

Enhance Your Earning Potential with Books by Alec Rowe

Having delved into "Words that Work", consider further expanding your knowledge and financial prospects with Alec Rowe's array of insightful books. Each title is tailored to boost your earning potential in various dynamic fields.

1. **"Six Figure Notary"**

    This book offers an in-depth guide to becoming a highly profitable notary and loan signing agent. It lays out a clear path to earning a substantial income in this niche market.

2. **"ChatGPT Millionaire by Alec Rowe"**

    Explore the revolutionary world of AI and its financial applications in this book. Rowe reveals how to harness ChatGPT and similar technologies to create new streams of income.

3. **"ChatGPT Money Machine"**

    Building on the concepts in "ChatGPT Millionaire", this book focuses on actionable strategies to monetize AI, turning cutting-edge tech into a reliable source of revenue.

4. **"Words that Work - Motivational Interviewing Mastery"**

    Enhance your communication skills with this guide on motivational interviewing. Mastering these techniques can lead to improved professional relationships and opportunities, thus increasing your earning potential.

5. **"Pass Your Journeyman Electrician Exam Study Guides"**

    These comprehensive guides are designed to help you excel in the Journeyman Electrician exam, a crucial step toward a lucrative career in the electrical trade.

6. **"Real Estate LLC Beginner's Launch Formula"**

    Start and protect your real estate business with my crash course on getting your real estate LLC up and running.

Alec Rowe's books are not just sources of information; they are gateways to higher earnings and professional growth. Whether you're looking to delve into the financial possibilities of AI, step into a profitable niche, or excel in a well-paying trade, these books provide the insights and guidance you need. Find Alec Rowe's complete library by clicking his name on the platform you purchased this book to access his author page, or searching his name.

Take the next step in your financial journey today!

Explore More from Jane Kennedy

If you found "Words that Work" insightful, you may be interested in exploring other books by Alec's co-author and editor, Jane Kennedy. Each book is crafted with the same dedication to providing valuable, transformative information.

1. **"Eat Good, Look Good, Feel Great: Healthy Eating for Beginners"**

   Dive into the world of healthy eating without sacrificing flavor. This newbie-friendly guide offers practical tips to lose weight, feel great, and dine like a dietician.

2. **"PCOS: The New Science of Completely Reversing Symptoms While Restoring Hormone Balance"**

   Discover groundbreaking approaches to managing PCOS, focusing on restoring hormonal balance, mental health, and fertility.

3. **"The PCOS Diet"**

   Tailored dietary strategies to help manage PCOS symptoms effectively, focusing on nutrition and wellness.

4. **"EMDR Revolution - 7 Guided EMDR Sessions"**

   An innovative approach to emotional healing, offering guided EMDR sessions to help you navigate and resolve deep-seated issues.

5. **"Stop Overthinking"**

   Tackle the habit of overthinking with practical strategies and insights, leading to a more relaxed and productive mindset.

6. **"Stop Overthinking Your Relationship!"**

   This book specifically addresses overthinking within relationships, offering guidance to foster healthier, more fulfilling connections.

7. **"The Sweet Escape: Sugar Detox for Beginners"**

   A beginner-friendly guide to reducing sugar intake, helping you embark on a healthier lifestyle with sustainable dietary changes.

Each of these books offers unique insights and practical advice, tailored to help you in different aspects of your health and well-being. Whether you're looking to enhance your diet, manage specific health conditions, or improve your mental health, Jane Kennedy's library has something for you. Find her full library by clicking on her name on the platform where you purchased this book to be taken to her author page.

Happy Reading!

Do you ever find yourself constantly doubting your abilities, even if you have achieved great success?

It's like a voice in your head whispering that you're a fraud, that one day everyone will discover your true incompetence.

You're not alone.

You Are Not a Fraud! By Jane Kennedy delves into the depths of **IMPOSTER SYNDROME,** providing strategies and insights to help you break free from the shackles of self-doubt and embrace your true potential.

Picture this: You're sitting in a meeting, surrounded by highly accomplished individuals, and you can't help but feel like a fraud. The fear of being exposed gnaws at you, causing anxiety and self-sabotage. But it doesn't have to be this way. Through relatable stories and practical advice, this book will empower you to challenge those negative thoughts, recognize your true worth, and develop unshakable confidence.

In this insightful guide, you will:

- Learn about the different types of imposters and the underlying causes of imposter syndrome

- Discover effective strategies to overcome self-doubt and cultivate a healthy sense of self-worth

- Gain practical tips for recognizing and challenging negative thoughts and beliefs about yourself

- Develop self-compassion and embrace your unique strengths and accomplishments

- Unleash your full potential and achieve the success you deserve

Don't let imposter syndrome hold you back from reaching your full potential.

Unmask the truth and break free from the cycle of self-doubt. Embrace the strategies and insights in this book, and step into a future where you confidently embrace your true abilities. Your journey to self-acceptance begins now. Find You are Not a Fraud! Escape Imposter Syndrome for Good and the rest of Jane Kennedy and Alec Rowe's respective libraries by searching for their names or clicking their author names to find their author pages on the platform you purchased Words that Work.

Thanks again for reading!

References

Aakash. (2023, March 31). *What is psychological change? – Everything you need to know*. Mantra Care. https://mantracare.org/therapy/what-is-psychological-change/

Adult obesity. (2016, April 14). Harvard T.H. Chan School of Public Health. https://www.hsph.harvard.edu/obesity-prevention-source/obesity-trends-original/obesity-rates-worldwide/#References

Alexander, H. (2020, July 24). *5 barriers to diet change and how to overcome them*. MD Anderson Cancer Center. https://www.mdanderson.org/publications/focused-on-health/5-barriers-to-diet-change-and-how-to-overcome-them.h28-1593780.html

Alyssa. (2023, January 24). *How motivational interviewing can treat mental illness*. Banyan Treatment Centers. https://www.banyanmentalhealth.com/2018/06/01/how-motivational-interviewing-can-treat-mental-illness/

Amjad, Z. (2020, January 24). *Coaching vs. Mentoring vs. Training vs. Facilitation*. Linkedin. https://www.linkedin.com/pulse/coaching-vs-mentoring-training-facilitation-zeeshan-amjad

Andreev, I. (2023, June 17). *Continuous learning*. Valamis. https://www.valamis.com/hub/continuous-learning

Arloski, M. (n.d.). *Ten ways to coach through the barriers to change*. Real Balance. https://realbalance.com/ten-ways-to-coach-through-the-barriers-to-change-outer-barriers-to-lifestyle-improvement

Balfour, J. (2020, January 10). *Empathy in coaching and leadership.* Bailey Balfour Asia Pacific. https://baileybalfour.com/empathy-matters-in-coaching-and-in-leadership/

Barnes, G. (2021, December 22). *The psychology of change.* Roffey Park Institute. https://www.roffeypark.ac.uk/knowledge-and-learning-resources-hub/the-psychology-of-change/

Barrett, S. (2021). *Motivational Interviewing: Facilitating behaviour change.* Don't Forget the Bubbles. https://dontforgetthebubbles.com/motivational-interviewing-facilitating-behaviour-change/

Batista, E. (2015, February 18). *How great coaches ask, listen, and empathize.* Harvard Business Review. https://hbr.org/2015/02/how-great-coaches-ask-listen-and-empathize

Bhat, A. (2023, October 19). *Open-ended questions: Examples & advantages.* QuestionPro. https://www.questionpro.com/blog/what-are-open-ended-questions/

Blackbyrn, S. (2024, January 4). *How to use affirmations in coaching.* Coach Foundation. https://coachfoundation.com/blog/coaching-affirmations/#1-definition-of-affirmations-and-overview-of-coaching-

Body image and diets. (n.d.-a). Better Health Channel. https://www.betterhealth.vic.gov.au/health/healthyliving/body-image-and-diets

Boitano, M. (2021, December 8). *The dietitian's guide to motivational interviewing.* Well Resourced Dietitian. https://wellresourced.com/motivational-interviewing-nutrition/

Bolter, H. (2022, September 5). *Just what is the relationship between stages of change & motivational interviewing.* Motivational Interviewing Blog. https://blog.micenterforchange.com/just-what-is-the-relationship-between-stages-of-change-motivational-interviewing/

Booth, F. W., Roberts, C. K., & Laye, M. J. (2012). Lack of exercise is a major cause of chronic diseases. *Comprehensive Physiology*, 1143–1211. https://doi.org/10.1002/cphy.c110025

Boutin, C. (2023, July 19). *9 key ingredients for a successful coaching relationship*. Paperbell. https://paperbell.com/blog/coaching-relationship/

Carl R. Rogers, on becoming a person (1961). (n.d.). Panarchy.org. https://www.panarchy.org/rogers/person.html

Cascio, C. N., O'Donnell, M. B., Tinney, F. J., Lieberman, M. D., Taylor, S. E., Strecher, V. J., & Falk, E. B. (2015). Self-affirmation activates brain systems associated with self-related processing and reward and is reinforced by future orientation. *Social Cognitive and Affective Neuroscience*, *11*(4), 621–629. https://doi.org/10.1093/scan/nsv136

Celestine, N. (2019, April 9). *4 ways to improve and increase self-efficacy*. PositivePsychology.com. https://positivepsychology.com/3-ways-build-self-efficacy/#4-ways-to-increase-self-efficacy

Century City. (2018, November 8). *The role of empathy and sympathy in coaching*. Gloveworx. https://www.gloveworx.com/blog/empathy-sympathy-in-coaching/

Cherry, K. (2023, February 27). *Self efficacy and why believing in yourself matters*. Verywell Mind. https://www.verywellmind.com/what-is-self-efficacy-2795954

Cherry, K. (2023, March 15). *What is resilience?* Verywell Mind. https://www.verywellmind.com/characteristics-of-resilience-2795062

Chodipilli, K. (2022, November 9). The power of questions – facilitation vs coaching. *Leadership Tribe US*. https://leadershiptribe.com/blog/the-power-of-questions-facilitation-vs-coaching

Comparing facilitation, coaching, mentoring and teaching. (n.d.). Scrum.org. https://www.scrum.org/resources/comparing-facilitation-coaching-mentoring-and-teaching

Costa, C. (2022, May 25). *6 ways to track and measure your fitness goals*. American Home Fitness. https://americanhomefitness.com/blogs/news/6-ways-to-track-and-measure-your-fitness-goals

Creating the perfect life coach session. (2023, June 14). *Practice*. https://practice.do/blog/life-coach-session

Cullen, E. (2023, March 15). *How to ask open-ended questions: 20 examples*. Mentimeter. https://www.mentimeter.com/blog/stand-out-get-ahead/how-to-create-open-ended-questions

Dean, S., Britt, E., Bell, E., Stanley, J., & Collings, S. (2016). Motivational interviewing to enhance adolescent mental health treatment engagement: a randomized clinical trial. *Psychological Medicine, 46*(9), 1961–1969. https://doi.org/10.1017/s0033291716000568

DeFelice, R. (2022, November 17).*The complete guide to transition coaching*. Life Coach Spotter. https://www.lifecoachspotter.com/transition-coach/

Derler, A., & Ray, J. (2019, December 12). *Why change is so hard — and how to deal with It*. NeuroLeadership Institute. https://neuroleadership.com/your-brain-at-work/growth-mindset-deal-with-change

Developing a growth mindset about people's ability to change. (2023, December 18). Greater Good in Education. https://ggie.berkeley.edu/practice/developing-a-growth-mindset-about-peoples-ability-to-change/

Diller, S. J., Mühlberger, C., Löhlau, N., & Jonas, E. (2021). How to show empathy as a coach: The effects of coaches' imagine-self versus imagine-other empathy on the client's self-change and coaching outcome. *Current Psychology, 42*(14), 11917–11935. https://doi.org/10.1007/s12144-021-02430-y

Exercise & fitness: Facts & statistics. (n.d.). RxResource.org. https://www.rxresource.org/fitness/exercise-and-fitness-facts-and-statistics.html

Finley, J. A. (2023, August 29). *Business isn't just about numbers and revenue*. Medium. https://medium.com/bts-magazine-behind-the-success/business-isnt-just-about-numbers-and-revenue-ac12fbd0f776

5 essential components to build a strong coach-client relationship. (2023, March 15). Simply.Coach. https://simply.coach/infographics/5-essential-components-to-build-a-strong-coach-client-relationship/

Flegal, K. M., Carroll, M. D., Kit, B. K., & Ogden, C. L. (2012). Prevalence of obesity and trends in the distribution of body mass index among US adults, 1999-2010. *JAMA, 307*(5), 491. https://doi.org/10.1001/jama.2012.39

Florez, G. (2020, July 4). *Understanding your client's core motivations.* American Council on Exercise. https://www.acefitness.org/resources/pros/expert-articles/7598/understanding-your-client-s-core-motivations/

14 coaches share their most notable client success stories. (2022, August 23). Forbes. https://www.forbes.com/sites/forbescoachescouncil/2022/08/23/14-coaches-share-their-most-notable-client-success-stories/

Geerling, R., Browne, J. L., Holmes-Truscott, E., Furler, J., Speight, J., & Mosely, K. (2019). Positive reinforcement by general practitioners is associated with greater physical activity in adults with type 2 diabetes. *BMJ Open Diabetes Research & Care, 7*(1), e000701. https://doi.org/10.1136/bmjdrc-2019-000701

Giles, L. (2018, April 3). *Eliciting change talk: Infusing Motivational interviewing with intentionality.* IRETA. https://ireta.org/eliciting-change-talk-infusing-motivational-interviewing-with-intentionality/

Griffith L. J. (2008). The psychiatrist's guide to motivational interviewing. *Psychiatry (Edgmont (Pa. : Township)), 5*(4), 42–47.

Hagley, K. (2023, February 4). *The importance of visualization and positive self-talk in track & field.* The Track Closet. https://thetrackcloset.com/blog2/2020/1/15/the-importance-of-visualization-and-positive-self-talk-in-track-amp-field

Hainsworth, E. (2023, December 14). *Motivational interviewing and why it's important?* Carepatron. https://www.carepatron.com/guides/motivational-interviewing

Harnessing right speech: The transformative power of words for a brighter tomorrow. (2023, October 23). The Foundation for Developing Compassion and Wisdom. https://www.compassionandwisdom.org/blog/2023/8/25/harnessing-right-speech-the-transformative-power-of-words-for-a-brighter-tomorrow

Hartney, E. (2023, November 14). *Understanding motivational interviewing.* Verywell Mind. https://www.verywellmind.com/what-is-motivational-interviewing-22378

Healthy eating: Overcoming barriers to change. (n.d.). HealthLink BC. https://www.healthlinkbc.ca/healthy-eating-physical-activity/food-and-nutrition/eating-habits/healthy-eating-overcoming

Hoeg, N. (2023, October 26). *Motivational interviewing.* Addiction Center. https://www.addictioncenter.com/treatment/motivational-interviewing/

How can you help clients with low self-efficacy in career counseling? (2023, August 18). Linkedin. https://www.linkedin.com/advice/1/how-can-you-help-clients-low-self-efficacy-career

How coaches can create safe environments in their team. (n.d.). TeamSnap. https://www.teamsnap.com/blog/general-sports/how-coaches-can-create-safe-environments-in-their-teams

How do you create a safe and trusting space for coaching and mentoring conversations? (2023, May 24). Linkedin. https://www.linkedin.com/advice/0/how-do-you-create-safe-trusting-space-coaching

How do you integrate new skills into your practice? (2023, August 11). Linkedin. https://www.linkedin.com/advice/3/how-do-you-integrate-new-skills-your-practice

How do you measure the outcomes and impacts of MI? (2023, March 30). Linkedin. https://www.linkedin.com/advice/1/how-do-you-measure-outcomes-impacts-mi

How do you use motivational interviewing to facilitate change in coaching? (2023, December 8). Linkedin. https://www.linkedin.com/advice/1/how-do-you-use-motivational-interviewing-facilitate

How does body image affect mental health? (2022, May 26). Integris Health. https://integrisok.com/resources/on-your-health/2022/may/how-does-body-image-affect-mental-health

Jerome, A. (2020, August 28). *The top 10 excuses for not exercising and how to overcome them.* Sport and Recreation. https://sport.port.ac.uk/news-events-and-blogs/blogs/health-and-fitness/the-top-10-excuses-for-not-exercising-and-how-to-overcome-them

Kamya, H. (2012, April). *Motivational interviewing and field instruction: The FRAMES model.* Field Educator Journal. https://fieldeducator.simmons.edu/article/motivational-interviewing-and-field-instruction-the-frames-model/

Kanaga, N. (2021, April 1). *7 ways personal trainers can increase client motivation.* Virtuagym. https://business.virtuagym.com/blog/increase-client-motivation/

Kristin. (2020, October 15). *Stop managing and start coaching.* Baird Group. https://baird-group.com/stop-managing-and-start-coaching/

Kristin. (2021, May 17). *Stop fixing & start coaching.* Baird Group. https://baird-group.com/stop-fixing-start-coaching/

Latif, S. (2021, May 19). *Is motivational interviewing effective? A look at 5 benefits.* PositivePsychology.com. https://positivepsychology.com/motivational-interviewing-effectiveness/

Lonczak, H. S. (2021, May 29). *How to build rapport with clients: 18 examples & questions*. PositivePsychology.com. https://positivepsychology.com/rapport-building/#google_vignette

Lonczak, H. S., PhD. (2023, September 19). *36 motivational interviewing quotes to inspire your clients*. PositivePsychology.com. https://positivepsychology.com/motivational-interviewing-quotes/

Madson, M. B., Mohn, R. S., Schumacher, J. A., & Landry, A. S. (2015). Measuring client experiences of motivational interviewing during a lifestyle intervention. *Measurement and Evaluation in Counseling and Development, 48*(2), 140–151. https://doi.org/10.1177/0748175614544687

Marker, I., & Norton, P. J. (2018). The efficacy of incorporating motivational interviewing to cognitive behavior therapy for anxiety disorders: A review and meta-analysis. *Clinical Psychology Review, 62*, 1–10. https://doi.org/10.1016/j.cpr.2018.04.004

Martin, K. (2016, May 10). *6 ways to coach through transitions*. Blanchard LeaderChat. https://leaderchat.org/2016/05/10/6-ways-to-coach-through-transitions/

Motivational interviewing. (n.d.). Physiopedia. https://www.physio-pedia.com/Motivational_Interviewing

Motivational Interviewing: A patient-centered approach to elicit positive behavior change. (n.d.). DentalCare.com. https://www.dentalcare.com/en-us/ce-courses/ce381/components-of-mi

Motivational interviewing: Eliciting change talk and giving advice. (n.d.). The Homeless Hub. https://www.homelesshub.ca/resource/motivational-interviewing-eliciting-change-talk-and-giving-advice

Motivational interviewing for diet, exercise and weight. (n.d.). Yale Rudd Center for Food Policy and Obesity.

https://media.ruddcenter.uconn.edu/PDFs/MotivationalIntervie wing.pdf

Motivational interviewing for substance abuse. (2023, August 24). Vista Taos. https://www.vistataos.com/motivational-interviewing-for-substance-abuse/

Motivational interviewing: History, how it works, effectiveness. (2023, January 18). The Human Condition. https://thehumancondition.com/motivational-interviewing-overview/

Motivational interviewing (MI). (2024, January 11). PsychDB. https://www.psychdb.com/psychotherapy/mi

Motivational interviewing: Open questions, affirmation, reflective listening, and summary reflections (OARS). (1984). The Homeless Hub. https://www.homelesshub.ca/resource/motivational-interviewing-open-questions-affirmation-reflective-listening-and-summary

Motivational interviewing: Stages of change. (2023, November 15). Recovery First Treatment Center. https://recoveryfirst.org/therapy/motivational-interviewing/stages-of-change/

Motivational interviewing: Talking with someone struggling with opioid use disorder. (2021, June 11). Providers Clinical Support System. https://pcssnow.org/courses/motivational-interviewing-talking-with-someone-struggling-with-oud/

Moyers, T. B. (2004). History and happenstance: How motivational interviewing got its start. *Journal of Cognitive Psychotherapy, 18*(4), 291–298. https://doi.org/10.1891/jcop.18.4.291.63999

Nasm, T. S. (2020, August 25). *Reasons why people don't exercise.* Exercise.com. https://www.exercise.com/learn/why-do-people-not-exercise/

Oliver, H. (2023, March 23). *The science and art of reflecting, summarising and paraphrasing.* Coach Advancement by Tracy Sinclair. https://tracysinclair.com/reflecting-summarising-and-paraphrasing/

Overcoming client diet struggles: Breaking down barriers. (2019, February 25). *ISSA*. https://www.issaonline.com/blog/post/overcoming-client-diet-struggles-breaking-down-barriers

Ozbay, F., Johnson, D. C., Dimoulas, E., Morgan, C. A., Charney, D., & Southwick, S. (2007). Social support and resilience to stress: from neurobiology to clinical practice. *Psychiatry (Edgmont (Pa. : Township))*, *4*(5), 35–40.

Padgett, C. (2019, March 1). *How to enhance self-efficacy and resilience in your clients*. American Council on Exercise. https://www.acefitness.org/continuing-education/certified/march-2019/7222/how-to-enhance-self-efficacy-and-resilience-in-your-clients/

Physical activity - How to get active when you are busy. (n.d.-b). Better Health Channel. https://www.betterhealth.vic.gov.au/health/healthyliving/Physical-activity-how-to-get-active-when-you-are-busy

Prichard, D. (2023, October 3). *36 Strategies to motivate, celebrate, and engage your fitness members*. Mindbody. https://www.mindbodyonline.com/business/education/blog/34-best-ways-to-keep-your-fitness-members-motivated

Primeau, M. (2021, September 15). *Your powerful, changeable mindset*. Stanford Report. https://news.stanford.edu/report/2021/09/15/mindsets-clearing-lens-life

Readiness ruler. (2010). Center for Evidence-Based Practices. https://case.edu/socialwork/centerforebp/resources/readiness-ruler

Reinauer, C., Viermann, R., Förtsch, K., Linderskamp, H., Warschburger, P., Holl, R. W., Staab, D., Minden, K., Muche, R., Domhardt, M., Baumeister, H., & Meißner, T. (2018). Motivational interviewing as a tool to enhance access to mental health treatment in adolescents with chronic medical conditions and need for psychological support (COACH-MI): study protocol for a clusterrandomised controlled trial. *Trials*, *19*(1). https://doi.org/10.1186/s13063-018-2997-5

Ren, L., Xu, Y., Guo, X., Zhang, J., Wang, H., Lou, X., Liang, J., & Tao, F. (2018). Body image as risk factor for emotional and behavioral problems among Chinese adolescents. *BMC Public Health*, *18*(1). https://doi.org/10.1186/s12889-018-6079-0

Rubak, S., Sandbaek, A., Lauritzen, T., & Christensen, B. (2005). Motivational interviewing: a systematic review and meta-analysis. *The British journal of general practice : the journal of the Royal College of General Practitioners*, *55*(513), 305–312

Saulsbery, A. (n.d.). *Ambivalence: Definition, examples, & tips*. The Berkeley Well-Being Institute. https://www.berkeleywellbeing.com/ambivalence.html

Schooler, N. (2022, September 28). *Continuous learning as a professional*. Legacy Media Hub. https://legacymediahub.com/continuous-learning-as-a-professional/

Schultz, J. S. (2021, January 1). *4 Principles of motivational interviewing to elicit change*. PositivePsychology.com. https://positivepsychology.com/motivational-interviewing-principles/

7 ways personal trainers can increase client motivation. (2023, April 19). Virtuagym. https://business.virtuagym.com/blog/increase-client-motivation/

Shaffer, J. A. (2013). Stages-of-change model. In *Springer eBooks* (pp. 1871–1874). https://doi.org/10.1007/978-1-4419-1005-9_1180

Sjöling, M., Lundberg, K., Englund, E., Westman, A., & Jong, M. C. (2011). Effectiveness of motivational interviewing and physical activity on prescription on leisure exercise time in subjects suffering from mild to moderate hypertension. *BMC Research Notes*, *4*(1). https://doi.org/10.1186/1756-0500-4-352

The skill of empathy in coaching. (2023, February 9). The Coaching Room. https://thecoachingroom.com.au/blog/the-skill-of-empathy-in-coaching/

Spraul, T. (2020, August 25). *Reasons why people don't exercise*. Exercise.com. https://www.exercise.com/learn/why-do-people-not-exercise/

Staff, L. E. (2023, October 11). *What is active listening?* Center for Creative Leadership. https://www.ccl.org/articles/leading-effectively-articles/coaching-others-use-active-listening-skills/

Stages of change model. (n.d.). Loma Linda University. https://medicine.llu.edu/academics/resources/stages-change-model

Stanfield, J. T. (2017, October 31). *3 tips to help clients build self-efficacy for exercise.* American Council on Exercise. https://www.acefitness.org/resources/pros/expert-articles/6832/3-tips-to-help-clients-build-self-efficacy-for-exercise/

Stephan, T. (2021, August 6). *4 common barriers and how to help your nutrition coaching clients overcome them.* Dietitian Business Coaching. https://dietitianbusinesscoaching.com/blog/4-common-barriers-and-how-to-help-your-nutrition-coaching-clients-overcome-them/

Stoltzfus, D. (2022, August 29). *Overcoming barriers to healthy eating.* Nova Institute for Health. https://novainstituteforhealth.org/barriers-to-healthy-eating/

Summarising. (2021, September 15). Counselling Tutor. https://counsellingtutor.com/basic-counselling-skills/summarising/

Sutton, J. (2016, July 21). *Active listening: The art of empathetic conversation.* PositivePsychology.com. https://positivepsychology.com/active-listening/#what-is-active-listening

Sutton, J. (2021, October 12). *How to Improve your client's self-esteem in therapy: 7 tips.* PositivePsychology.com. https://positivepsychology.com/how-to-improve-self-esteem/

Sutton, J. (2022, August 11). *Motivation in counseling: 9 steps to engage your clients.* PositivePsychology.com. https://positivepsychology.com/motivation-counseling/

10 ways to build and maintain a healthy client relationship. (2022, July 18). Practice. https://practice.do/blog/ways-to-build-and-maintain-a-healthy-client-relationship

Thomas, C. (2023, July 13). *Coaching Corner - Change Talk vs Sustain Talk*. Adagio Fit. https://adagiofit.com/coaching-corner-change-talk-vs-sustain-talk/

Training guide: Motivational interviewing. (n.d.). Accend Services. http://accendservices.com/guides/trainingguide-motivationalinterviewing.php

12 strategies to attract clients to your coaching practice. (2016, August 8). Forbes. https://www.forbes.com/sites/forbescoachescouncil/2016/08/08/12-strategies-to-attract-clients-to-your-coaching-practice/?sh=ab4e175414cb

Understanding and addressing ambivalence. (2021, January 26). Vroon VDB. https://www.vroonvdb.com/understanding-and-addressing-ambivalence/

Understanding motivational interviewing. (n.d.). Motivational Interviewing Network of Trainers (MINT). https://motivationalinterviewing.org/understanding-motivational-interviewing

Using coaching skills to overcome client ambivalence. (2022, October 27). Spencer Institute Health, Holistic and Wellness Certifications. https://spencerinstitute.com/using-coaching-skills-to-overcome-client-ambivalence/

Vijeth, A. (2023, August 5). *Believe, achieve, succeed: How self-efficacy fuels achievement.* Linkedin. https://www.linkedin.com/pulse/believe-achieve-succeed-how-self-efficacy-fuels-arjun-vijeth

Waehner, P. (2022, April 13). *10 reasons you don't exercise.* Verywell Fit. https://www.verywellfit.com/top-reasons-you-dont-exercise-1229759

Walcott, M. (2023, July 6). *The power of mental strategies for peak sports performance.* The Rack. https://therackapc.com/the-power-of-mental-strategies-for-peak-sports-performance/

Wannen, J. (2016, June 29). *Health coach pro tip: Use affirmations to help clients develop new habits.* Primal Health Coach Institute.

https://www.primalhealthcoach.com/health-coach-pro-tip-use-affirmations-to-help-clients-develop-new-habits/

What are some of the differences and similarities between facilitation and coaching? (2024, January 3). Linkedin. https://www.linkedin.com/advice/0/what-some-differences-similarities-between-facilitation

What is active listening? (2023, October 11). Center for Creative Leadership. https://www.ccl.org/articles/leading-effectively-articles/coaching-others-use-active-listening-skills/

Why coaching with empathy is Important. (2022, December 20). Positive Coaching Alliance. https://positivecoach.org/the-pca-blog/why-coaching-with-empathy-is-important/

Zolfaghari, Z., Rezaee, N., Shakiba, M., & Navidian, A. (2018). Motivational interviewing–based training vs traditional training on the uptake of cervical screening: a quasi-experimental study. *Public Health, 160,* 94–99. https://doi.org/10.1016/j.puhe.2018.04.007

Made in the USA
Monee, IL
28 March 2025